WELCOME TO MERIDEE WINTERS CHORD QUEST!

Our brains are wired to learn by patterns – finally, a music book series that teaches that way (AND sure has fun doing it).

Welcome to Chord Quest – a kids' version of Meridee's cult-favorite Chord Crash Course series, which teaches key skills like chords, patterns, transposition, lead sheet reading and much, much more. Known for its playful comic-book design and trailblazing "learn by pattern and shape" approach, one of Chord Quest's most unique features is that it doesn't require you to read music. (Which is why students can learn chord progressions within just a few minutes and their favorite songs within just a few chapters.)

Psst! Are you a student of our All Star Piano Patterns Series? Chord Quest is a re-imagined reboot of those books. You can pick up right where you left off!

Here in book one, you'll portal from chapter to chapter as you learn skills, earn powers, play great music and work your way to a final challenge. (And save creativity, defeat Professor Perfecto and save some kids while you're at it.)

IN CHORD QUEST BOOK 1, YOU'LL LEARN:
- ★ Five Finger Patterns and Shapes
- ★ Intervals
- ★ Arpeggios
- ★ Chords
- ★ Famous Progressions
- ★ Pachelbel's Canon
- ★ Crossover Arpeggios
- ★ Major and Minor
- ★ Songwriting
- ★ And MORE!

EVIL VILLAIN

Head to mwfunstuff.com/cq1 for fun extras, online lesson info and more!

This book is a great standalone tool - OR an awesome finger exercise book to supplement any method!

YOU DON'T HAVE TO READ MUSIC. WE'RE SERIOUS.

The ability to read music is an incredible skill, and we're all for it. (Our Note Quest Game Book was created to specifically build that skill.) The Chord Quest series is designed to work for all levels, however, including those who can and can't read music. Music, including chords and arpeggios, is largely a beautiful combination of patterns. By learning and applying these patterns, anyone can play and write music. For those who can read music, this book works as a great supplement, adding higher level chord theory and comping skills to your existing skill set.

EXCLUSIVE TO THE MERIDEE WINTERS UNIVERSE
These tools will help you on your musical adventure:

KINESTHETIC KEYBOARDS will show you what to play.

QUANTUM QUIZZES will solidify what you've learned.

ROOT   SONGWRITING

SKILL BADGES will be earned each chapter.

THE LAB will give you a chance to experiment and create.

© 2020 Meridee Winters ® All Rights Reserved.

MERIDEE WINTERS™ CHORD QUEST POWERFUL PIANO LESSONS LEVEL 1: EASY KEYBOARD PATTERNS FOR BEGINNER KIDS

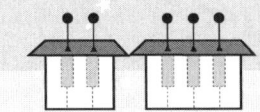

CHAPTER 1: WARM UP
Your Hands................................ (Pg. 2)
Finger Flash............................... (Pg. 3)
Black Keys................................. (Pg. 4)
White Keys................................. (Pg. 6)
1. Moonbeam Toccata In A............... (pg. 9)
Right Hand Warmup....................... (Pg. 10)
Left Hand Warmup........................ (Pg. 12)
2. RH Climb.................................. (pg. 13)
3. LH Climb.................................. (pg. 15)
4. Light Speed Fingers..................... (pg. 16)
Root Note Navigator..................... (Pg. 17)
Quantum Quiz............................. (Pg. 18)

CHAPTER 2: ARPEGGIOS

What is an Arpeggio?..................... (Pg. 20)
Left Hand Arpeggio....................... (Pg. 22)
5. Space Spider (RH)....................... (pg. 21)
Two-Handed Arpeggios.................. (Pg. 24)
6. Space Spider (LH)....................... (pg. 23)
Arpeggios Up and Down.................. (Pg. 24)
7. Astronomical Arpeggios................ (pg. 25)
8. Magnetic Malaguena................... (pg. 26)
9. Celestial Ballad.......................... (pg. 27)
10. Stars..................................... (pg. 27)
11. Waves................................... (pg. 29)
Quantum Quiz............................. (Pg. 30)

CHAPTER 3: CHORDS
PLAY BY SHAPE!
What is a chord?.......................... (Pg. 32)
12. Chord Scale Climb..................... (pg. 34)
Chord Scale Crash Course................ (Pg. 36)
13. Chord Scale Summit................... (pg. 37)
14. Chord Constellation................... (pg. 38)
15. Rock-et Chords........................ (pg. 38)
16. Malaguena Chord Combination 1..... (pg. 39)
17. Malaguena Chord Combination 1..... (pg. 39)
Deep Space Doo Wop..................... (Pg. 40)
18. Doo Wop Pattern 1.................... (pg. 41)
19. Doo Wop Pattern 2.................... (pg. 41)
Let's Experiment!......................... (Pg. 42)
Quantum Quiz............................. (Pg. 44)

CHAPTER 4: CHORD CONCERT: PACHELBEL

20. Pattern 1: Arpeggio, Arpeggio........ (pg. 46)
21. Pattern 2: Root, Arpeggio............. (pg. 47)
22. Pattern 3: Arpeggio, Chord........... (pg. 47)
23. Pattern 4: Chord, Arpeggio........... (pg. 48)
24. Pattern 5: Chord, Chord.............. (pg. 49)
Quantum Quiz............................. (Pg. 50)

CHAPTER 5: CROSSOVER ARPEGGIOS
What is a Crossover Arpeggio?.......... (Pg. 52)
25. Crossover Arpeggio Scale............ (pg. 53)
26. Malaguena Moondance................ (pg. 54)
27. Stargazer............................... (pg. 55)
28. Pachelbel Power-Up................... (pg. 56)
Quantum Quiz............................. (Pg. 58)

CHAPTER 6: INTERVALS
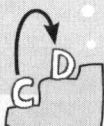
Seconds................................... (Pg. 60)
29. Toccata In Seconds.................... (pg. 61)
30. Waltz of Wonder...................... (pg. 61)
Melodic Thirds............................ (Pg. 62)
31. Pachelbel With Thirds................. (pg. 63)
Harmonic Thirds.......................... (Pg. 64)
32. Dreaming Clouds...................... (pg. 65)
33. Dreaming Improv..................... (pg. 65)
Fourths................................... (Pg. 66)
34. Space Chopper........................ (pg. 67)
Quantum Quiz............................. (Pg. 68)

© 2020 Meridee Winters ® All Rights Reserved.

CHAPTER 7: POWER CHORDS: FIFTHS
35. Dragon Warrior.................... (pg. 70)
36. Lunar Lightning .... (pg. 71)
37. Mysterious Moon .... (pg. 72)
38. Warrior Heart..................... (pg. 73)
Heart of Rock...................... (Pg. 74)
39. Heart Of Rock 1 .... (pg. 75)
40. Heart Of Rock 2 .... (pg. 75)
41. Heart Of Rock 3 .... (pg. 75)
Quantum Quiz..................... (Pg. 76)

CHAPTER 9: MAJOR MINOR CONCERTO
47. Major Minor Concerto: Arpeggios ..... (pg. 90)
48. Major Minor Concerto: Chords .... (pg. 92)
Reflect: See What You've Accomplished. (Pg. 94)

CHAPTER 8: MAJOR AND MINOR CHORDS
What is a Major Chord?............. (Pg. 78)
What is a Minor Chord? .... (Pg. 79)
42. Minor Chord Mash Up .... (pg. 80)
43. Major Chord Merriment............ (pg. 81)
Major to Minor..................... (Pg. 82)
44. Downward Shift .... (pg. 83)
Minor to Major..................... (Pg. 84)
45. Upward Bound .... (pg. 85)
46. Malaguena Masterpiece .... (pg. 86)
Quantum Quiz .... (Pg. 88)

CHORD QUEST TEST
Songwriting Lab .... (Pg. 98)
Write Down Your Creations! .... (Pg. 100)
Chord Quest Award................. (Pg. 102)

SNEAK PEEK: CHORD QUEST LEVEL 2.................... (Pg. 103)

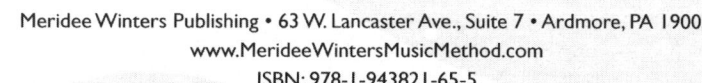

MERIDEE WINTERS™
CHORD QUEST: POWERFUL PIANO LESSONS LEVEL 1
EASY KEYBOARD PATTERNS FOR BEGINNER KIDS

© Copyright 2011, 2019, 2020 by Meridee Winters. All rights reserved.
Music compositions © Copyright 2003, 2011, 2019, 2020 by Meridee Winters. All rights reserved.

Meridee Winters Publishing • 63 W. Lancaster Ave., Suite 7 • Ardmore, PA 19003
www.MerideeWintersMusicMethod.com
ISBN: 978-1-943821-65-5

Meridee Winters: Music Composer, Author, and Art Director
Kate Capps: Editor, Creative Consultant, Music Engraving
Madé Dimas Wirawan: Illustrations
Sean Miller: Layout and Graphic Design, Additional Illustrations
Tatiana Tsitsura: Additional Graphic Design and Illustrations
Armand Alidio: Cover Design, Additional Illustrations, Additional Design
Krysta Bernhardt: Additional Design
Gabriel Rhopers: Creative Consultant; Peter Horst, Kaitlin Borden, Emily Cooley: Proofreading

CHAPTER 1

WARM UP

Even the most famous masters of space exploration, professional sports and popular music had to start at the very beginning and go step by step. Each one will tell you that the rewards are great – if you stick with it! What are the keys to success? Some say "never give up," "work on technique" or "practice every day," but they all know that the power to succeed is in their own hands.

Let's start training for success!

P.S. - If you recently completed Meridee's "Super Start! My First Piano Patterns" Book (on Planet Plunk!), you'll find this first chapter to be a breeze. Zip on through at warp speed or skip ahead! If this book is your first stop in the MW Musical Universe, this chapter will teach you the skills you need for a great start!

Keep an eye out for crystals! When you find one, color it in. They can often be found where creativity is plentiful. You'll need them later!

Warm Up

YOUR HANDS

Your hands and fingers hold the key to making music. Learning the number of each finger lets you know which one to play.

1 - 2 - 3 - 4 - 5

FINGER NUMBERS

In music, we use finger numbers to communicate which notes to play with which fingers. In piano music, the thumbs are finger number one, the index fingers are number two, and so on. That makes our pinkies finger number five! It's the same for both hands.

LABEL THE FINGER NUMBERS BELOW ☐ COMPLETE!

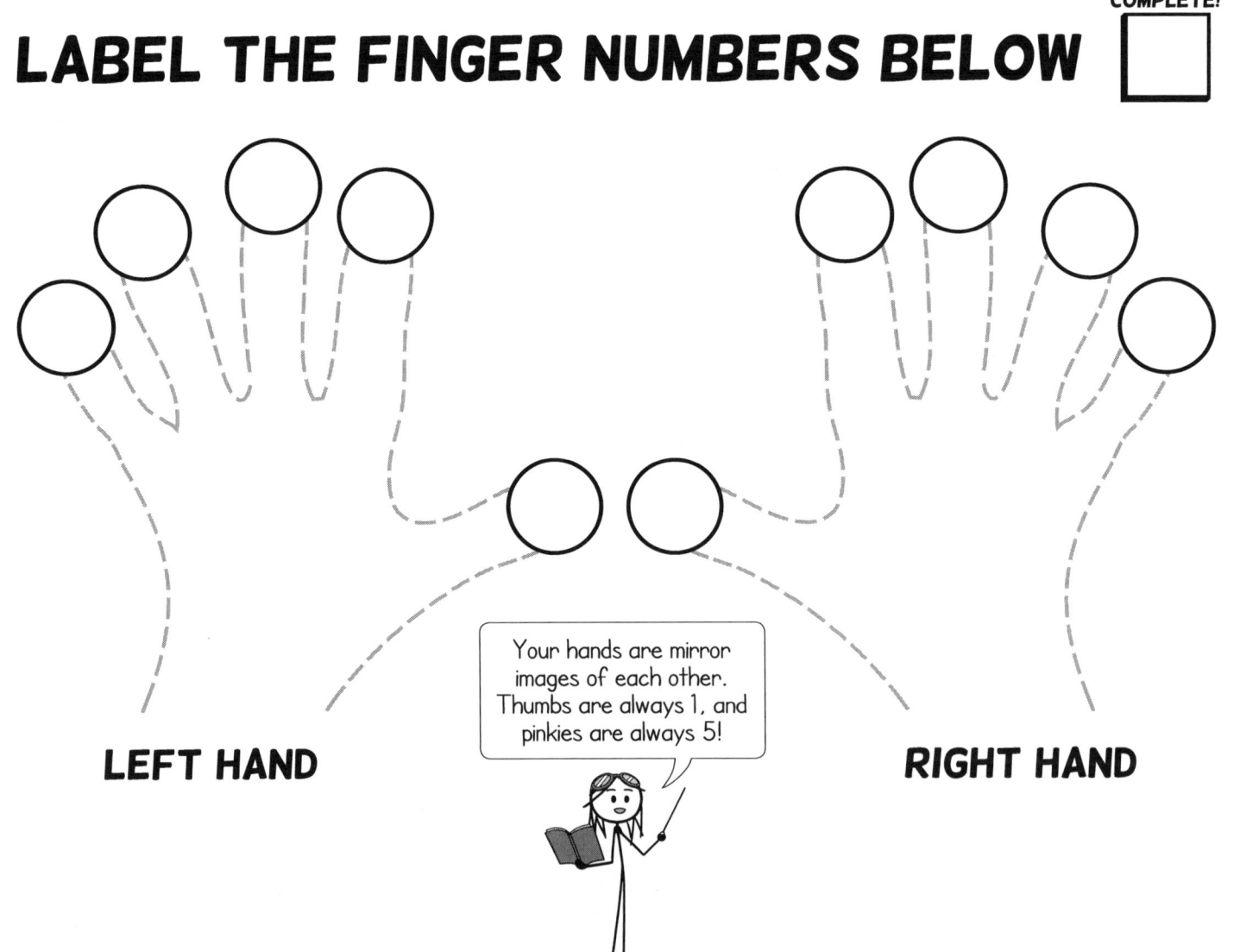

LEFT HAND   RIGHT HAND

Your hands are mirror images of each other. Thumbs are always 1, and pinkies are always 5!

Warm Up

FINGER FLASH

1. With your right hand, play the game by putting the correct finger number on each circle.
2. Repeat the game with your left hand.
3. For an extra challenge, time yourself. Keep revisiting the game to beat your own time!

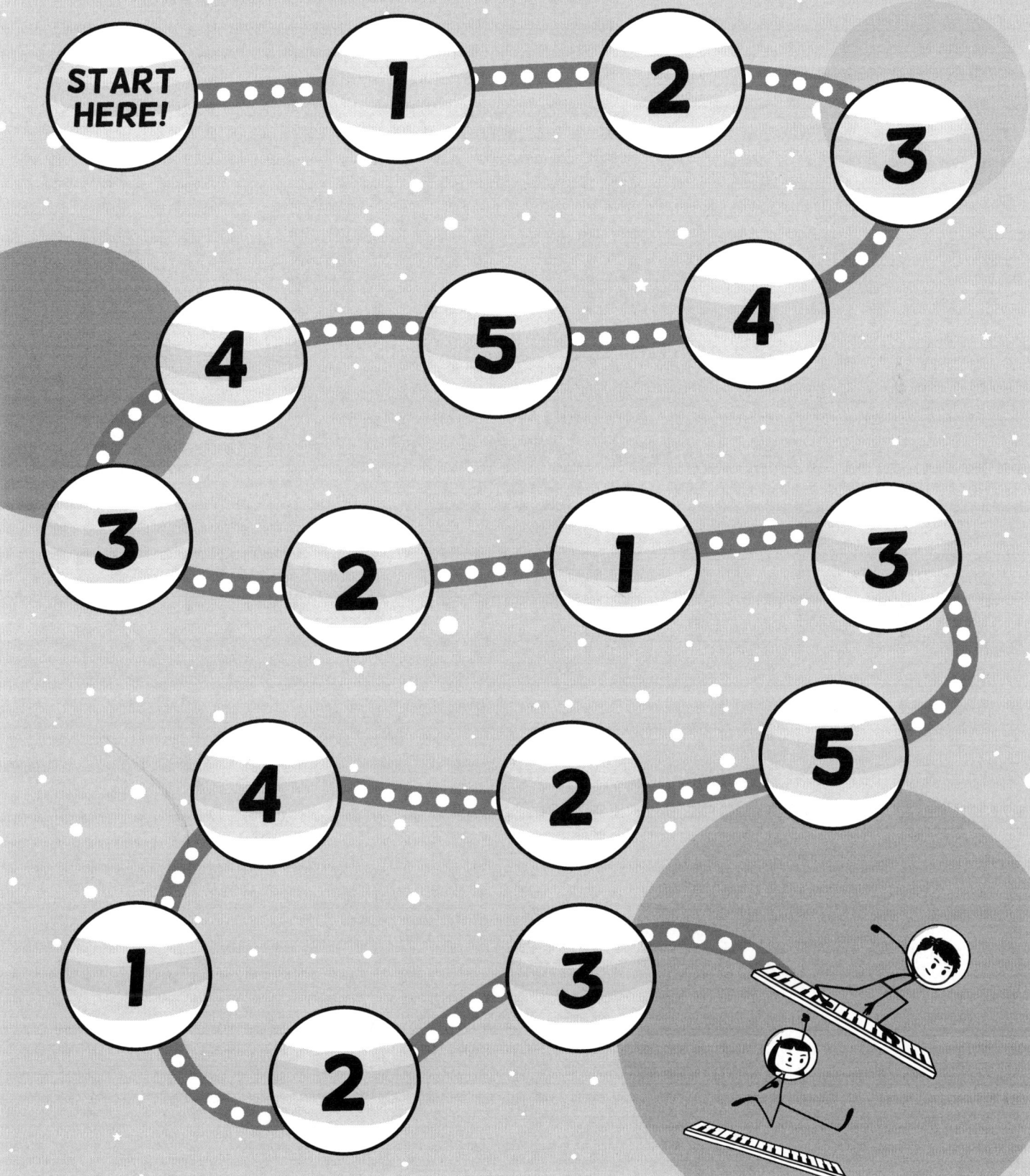

Warm Up

BLACK KEYS

The piano has black keys that come in sets of 2 and 3. Let's practice finding them!

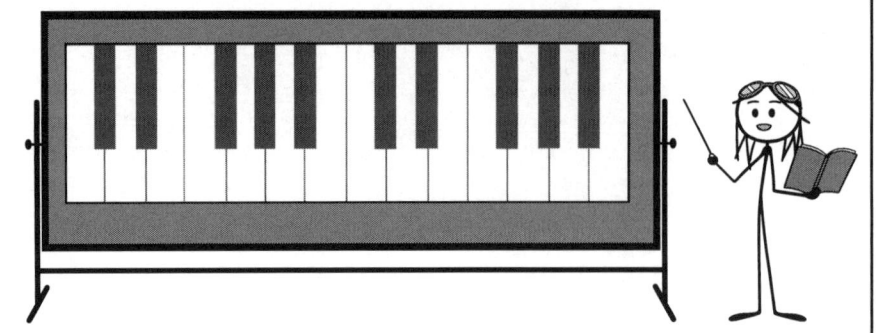

 **CIRCLE THEN PLAY ALL THE SETS OF 2 BLACK KEYS**

 COMPLETE!

 **CIRCLE THEN PLAY ALL THE SETS OF 3 BLACK KEYS**

 COMPLETE!

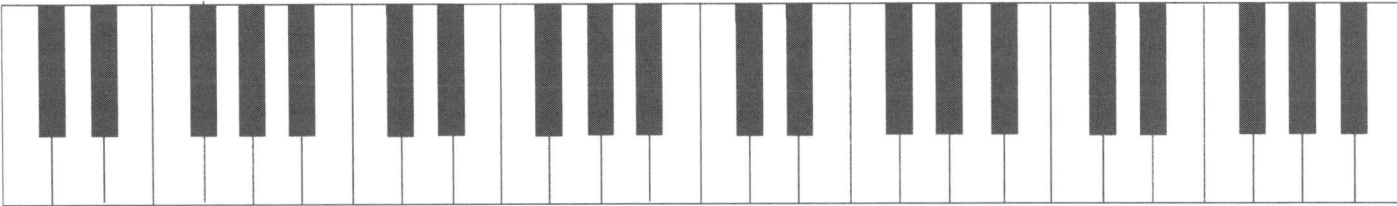

Warm Up

BLACK KEY JAM!

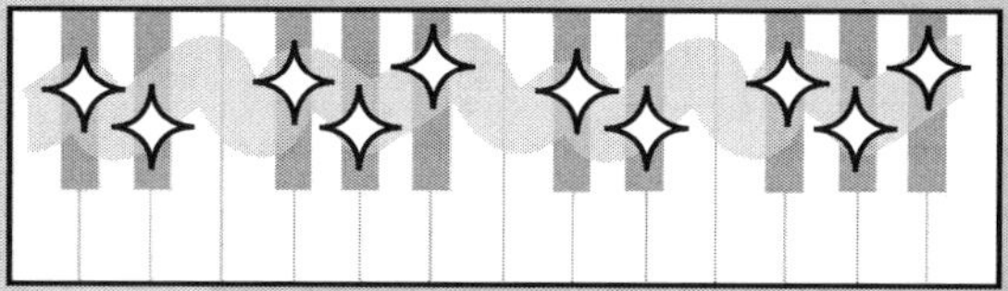

"Improvising" is making something up as you go - kind of like fingerpainting! Here, improvise by playing any black keys on the piano. Add a teacher duet part from below to make it extra amazing!

- EXPLORE WITH BLACK KEYS
- KEEP PLAYING
- GET INTO THE FLOW

Explore! There are no mistakes in jamming.

TEACHER DUET PARTS

JAZZY JAM

Tip! This part has a descending bass line, and the top notes stay the same for almost all of it!

PENTA JAM

Tip! Keep the pedal down and play peacefully. The five black keys form a pentatonic scale, which has its roots in the Far East.

Great exploring!

Warm Up

WHITE KEYS

Each of the seven white keys has a name that comes from the musical alphabet. Using the groups of black keys as markers can help find the notes.

The musical alphabet goes from A to G and then starts over again.

MUSICAL ALPHABET

Finish filling in the musical alphabet on the keyboard below.

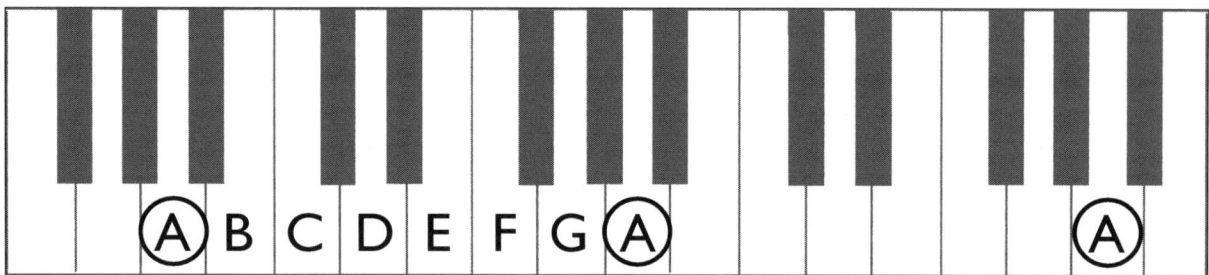

CIRCLE, LABEL AND PLAY

Start by labeling each A and then fill in the rest of the keyboard below. Start at the bottom of your piano keyboard and play and say each note all the way up!

SECRET TRICK! FOR REMEMBERING THE PIANO KEYS

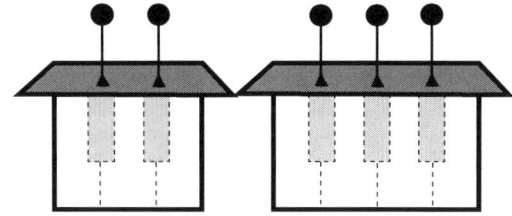

We've borrowed this tip from Meridee's Super Start Solar System books. Imagine there are two houses. One with 2 antennas (black keys) and one with 3 antennas (black keys).

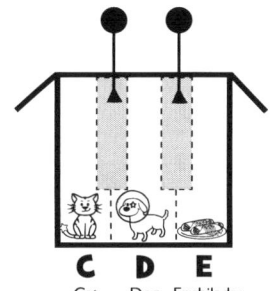

Let's look at the house with two antennas (two black keys). In the middle is a dog, but he also lives with a cat (on his left) and they LOVE enchiladas (on the right). Find the two "antennas" and think: Cat, Dog, Enchiladas: C, D, E!

COMPLETE!

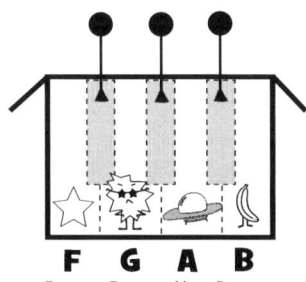

Now think of a house with three antennas (black keys). In this house lives a Famous Grumpy Alien, and he eats... Bananas! Find the sets of three "antennas" and think: Famous Grumpy Alien, Bananas - F, G, A, B!

COMPLETE!

MUSICAL METEORS

To play: Point to a meteor below. Find and play that note.
(Extra credit: find all instances of that note on the piano!)

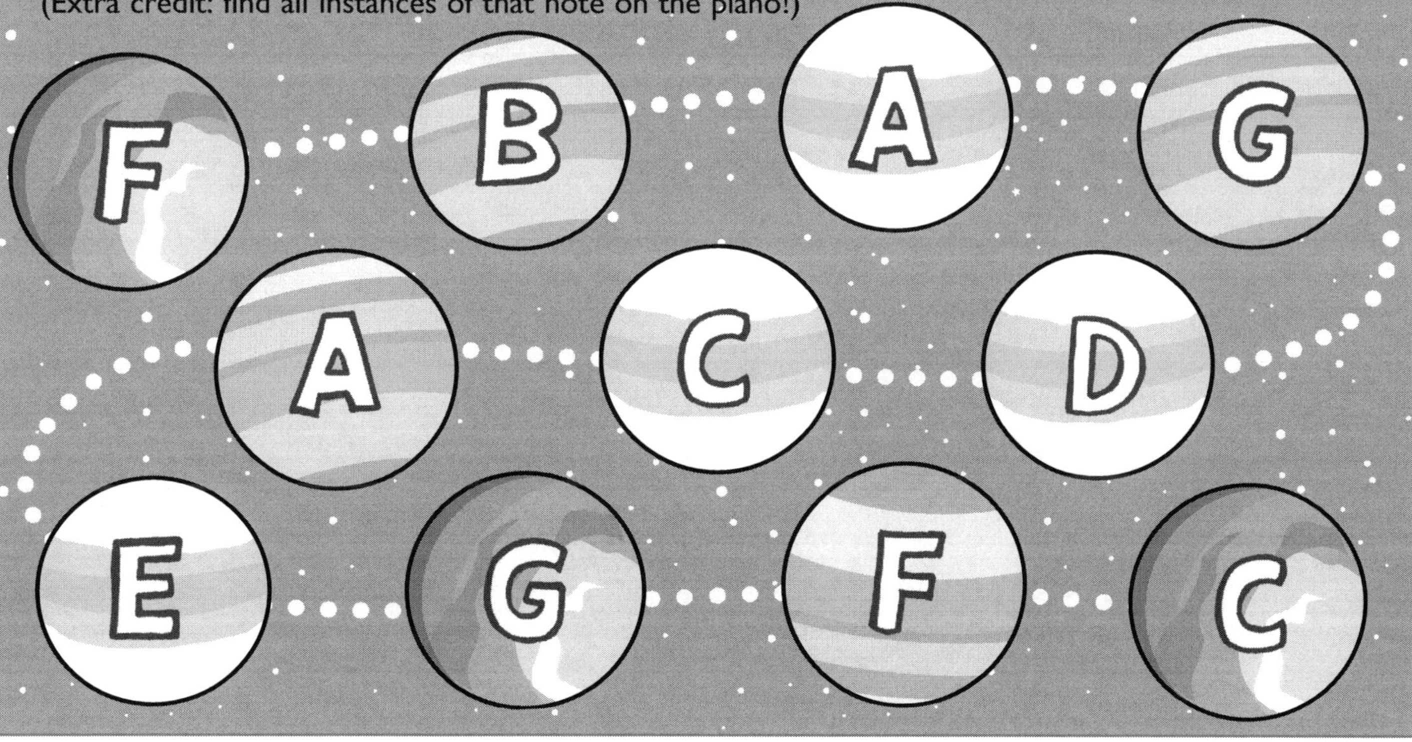

F B A G

A C D

E G F C

Warm Up

MOONBEAM TOCCATA

HOW TO PLAY:

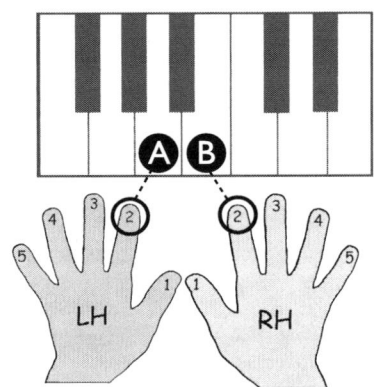

Play A with your left hand finger 2.

Then Play B (the note next to it) with your right hand finger 2.

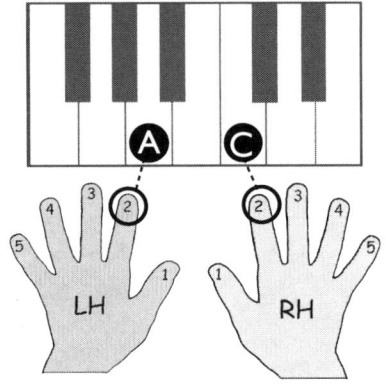

Left hand stays put! Play A with left hand finger 2 again.

Move your right hand up one note to play C with finger 2.

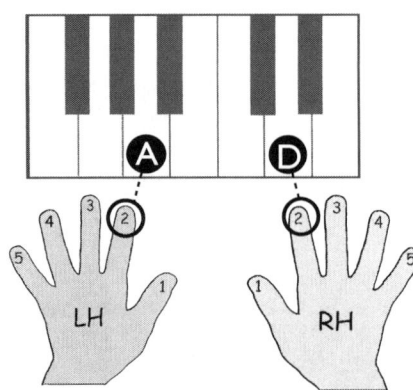

Left hand still stays put! Play A with left hand finger 2 again.

Move your right hand up another note and play D with finger 2.

Repeat this left-right pattern until your right hand reaches A!

TIP! Press down the right-most pedal on the piano as you play, or try an orchestra sound if using a keyboard!

1 MOONBEAM TOCCATA IN A

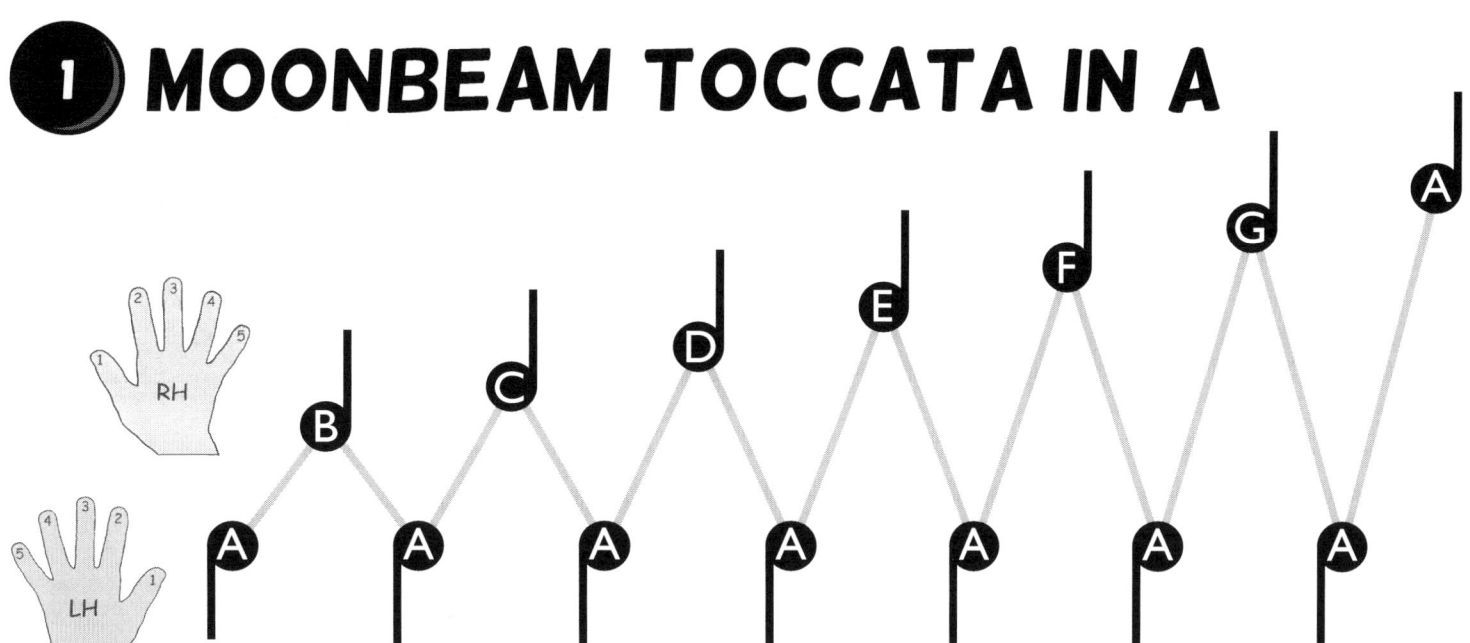

GET CREATIVE!

CREATIVITY

TRY GOING THE OTHER DIRECTION: RIGHT HAND STARTS ON A AND THE LEFT HAND MOVES DOWN ONE NOTE EACH TIME.

TRY YOUR OWN TOCCATA, STARTING ON A DIFFERENT NOTE OF THE SCALE.

TRY PLAYING SMOOTHLY AND SERENELY.

TRY PLAYING EACH NOTE TWICE: AA-BB-AA-CC AND SO ON.

TRY STARTING THE SONG QUIETLY, BUILDING TO A LOUD ENDING.

Warm Up

RIGHT HAND WARM UP

Press each key slowly and one at a time. Breathe and feel each finger as your hand makes its way up the piano!

1 - 2 - 3 - 4 - 5

 **PLAY EACH FINGER ONE AT A TIME...**

- Start with finger number 1 (thumb) on C. (C is the note to the left of the two black keys.)
- Then use finger number 2 to play the next note.
- Keep going until you run out of fingers.

1

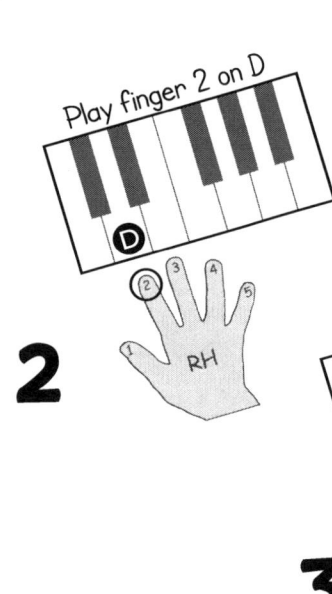

2

3

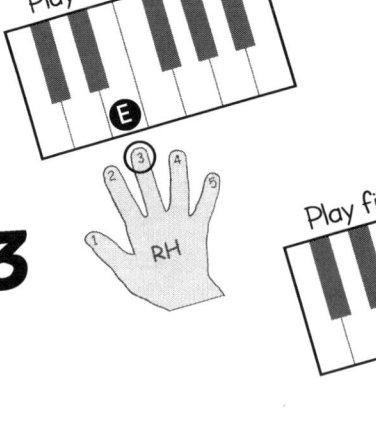

4

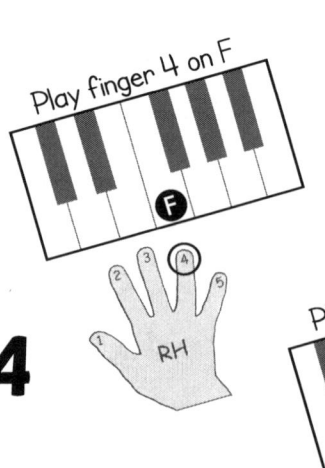

5

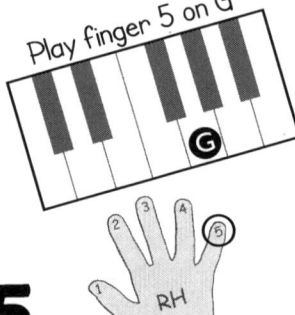

In this book, use the pictures to help you find notes and figure out the patterns.

STEP 2: LOOK AT THE SHAPE ON THE KEYBOARD AND STAFF

Here is what the pattern looks like on the keyboard.

Here is what the pattern looks like on the staff.

STEP 3: PRACTICE

Practice the right hand pattern until it is smooth. Say/think: "One, two, three, four, five."

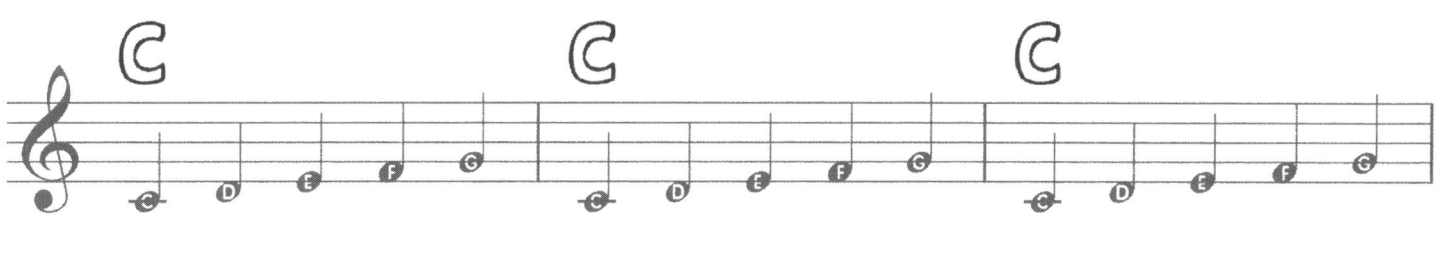

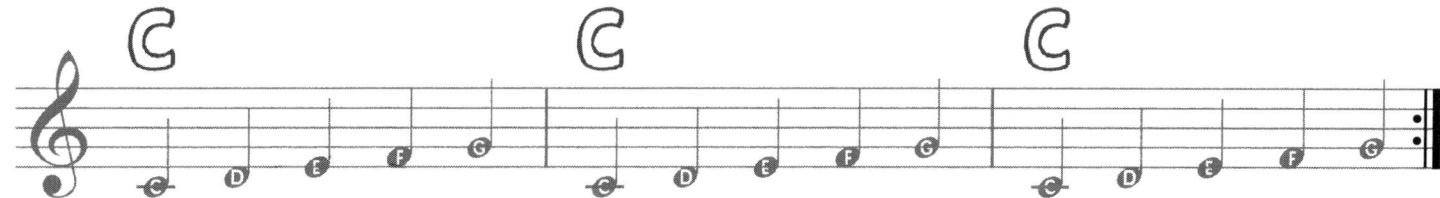

In music, like in sports, practice is important. Practice the pattern until it is smooth and even!

Warm Up

GET READY FOR RH CLIMB!

ON THE KEYS...

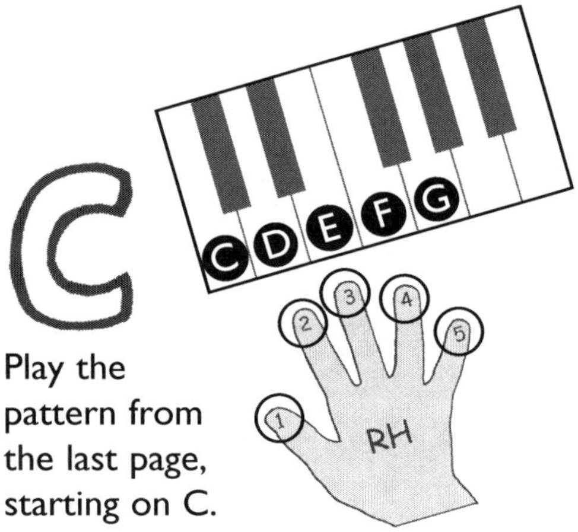

C Play the pattern from the last page, starting on C.

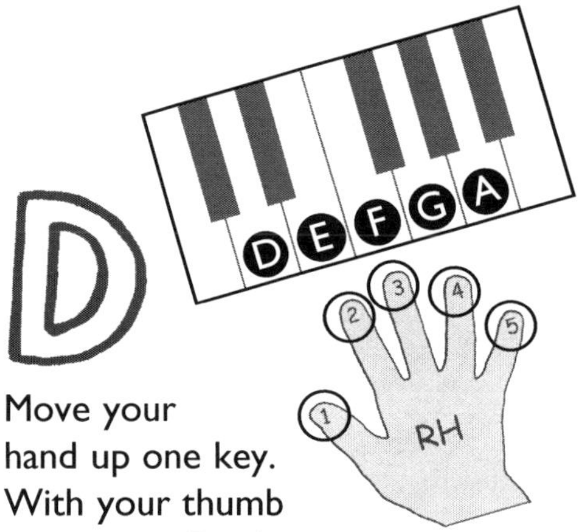

D Move your hand up one key. With your thumb starting on D, play fingers 1-2-3-4-5 again.

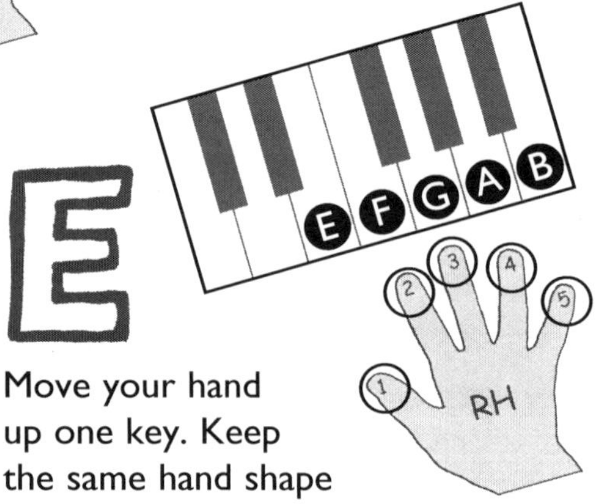

E Move your hand up one key. Keep the same hand shape as you play the pattern starting on E.

TIME TO STEP IT UP!

2 RH CLIMB

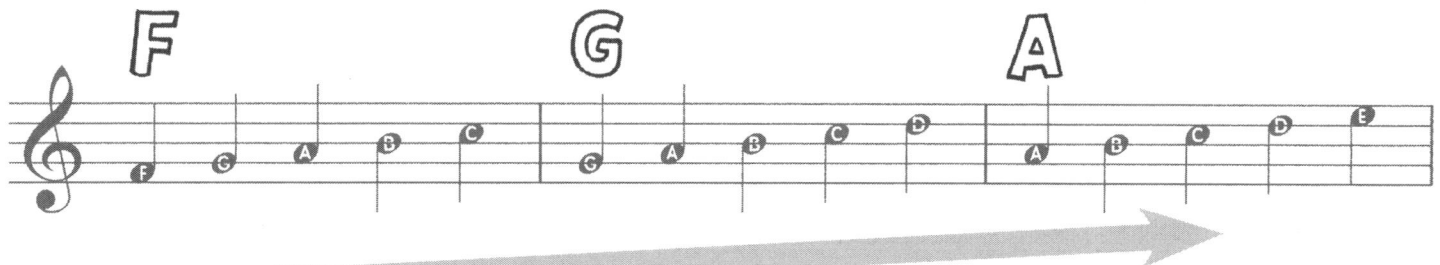

Warm Up

Now let's train your left hand.

LEFT HAND WARM UP

Starting with your left hand pinky, use each finger to step up the keys. Go slowly and be accurate. Most people find that playing with their left hand is challenging. That is normal. Masters never shy away from a challenge!

PLAY EACH FINGER ONE AT A TIME...

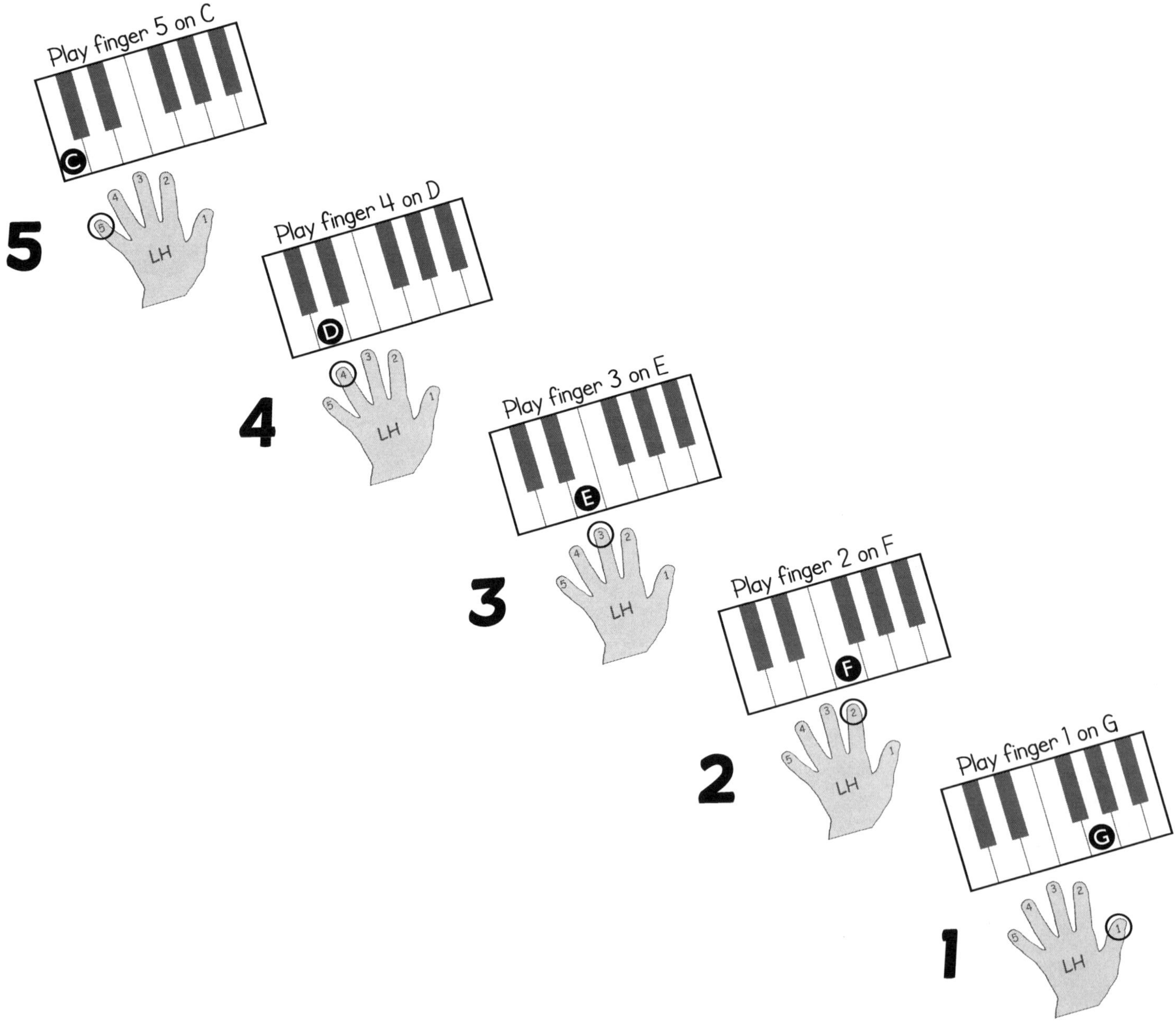

5 — Play finger 5 on C

4 — Play finger 4 on D

3 — Play finger 3 on E

2 — Play finger 2 on F

1 — Play finger 1 on G

Warm Up

TIME TO STEP IT UP!

3. LH CLIMB

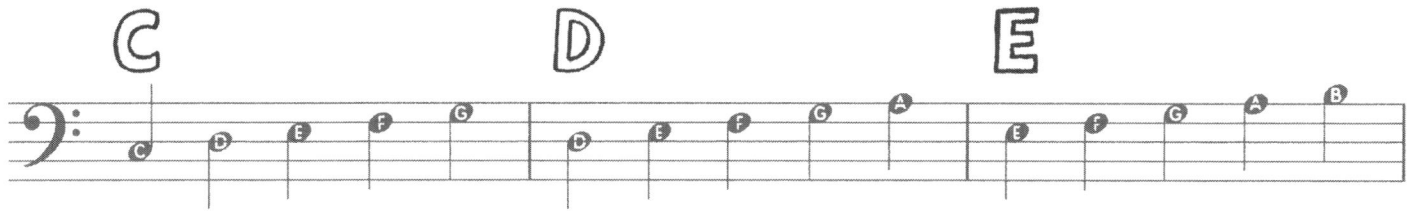

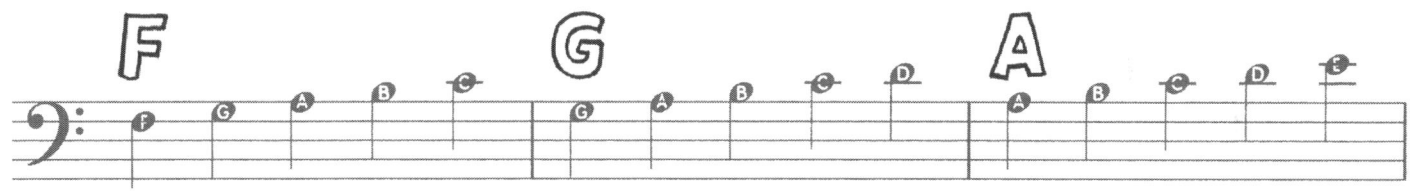

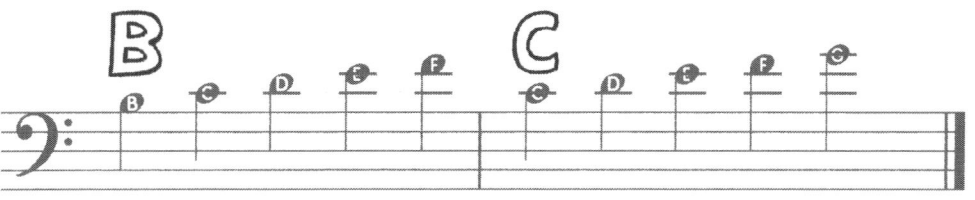

4 LIGHT SPEED FINGERS

Play the pattern starting on C.

Next, move your hand up one key and play the pattern with your thumb starting on D.

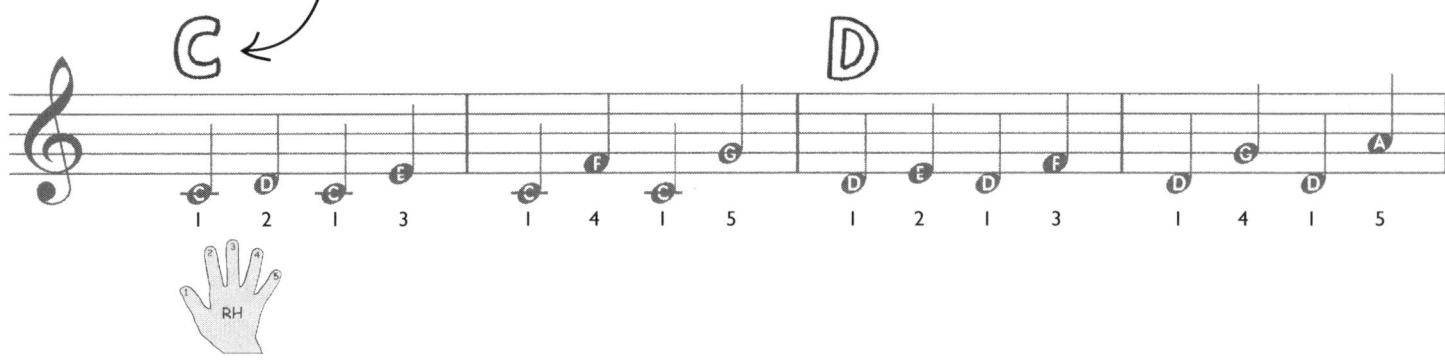

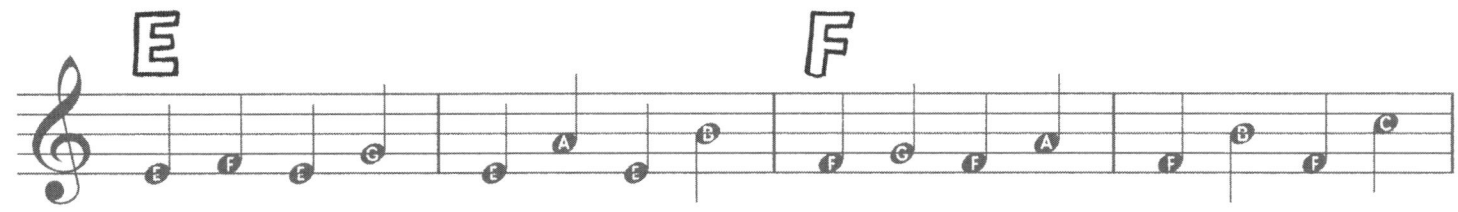

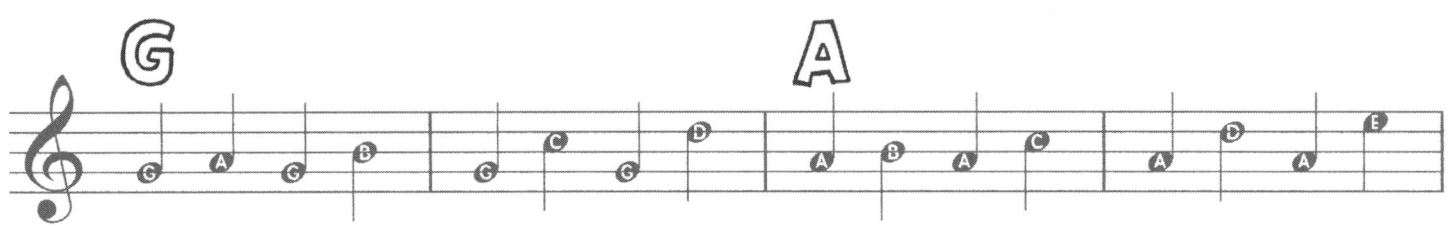

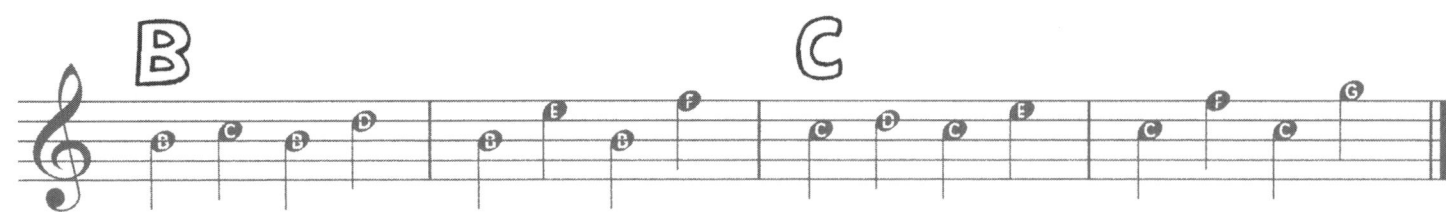

Say/think: "ONE-two, ONE-three, ONE-four, ONE-five!"

Warm Up

ROOT NOTE NAVIGATOR

A "root" note is the bottom note of a chord, arpeggio or pattern. (You'll learn chords and arpeggios soon!) When using your left hand, think of your pinky as an arrow targeting the root note. When using your right hand, think of your thumb as the arrow. Just move your "arrow" to the correct root note and the other fingers will fall into place!

ROOT

PATTERN 1:

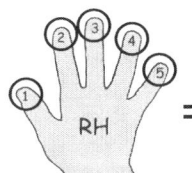

FINGERS = 1-2-3-4-5

PATTERN 2:

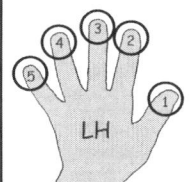

FINGERS = 5-4-3-2-1

PATTERN 3:

CREATE YOUR OWN!

WAYS TO PLAY!
- Point to any root note and play the pattern starting on that note.
- Use dice and roll to see which root note to use.
- Create your own!

Warm Up

QUANTUM QUIZ!

1 LABEL THE FINGER NUMBERS

2 LABEL THE NOTES

3 PLAY LIGHT SPEED FINGERS FROM MEMORY.

COMPLETE! ☐

COMMAND CENTER

Pattern Powers

 ROOT	 ARPEGGIO
 POWER PROGRESSION	 CHORDS
 PROGRESSION	 POWER PROGRESSION
 CROSSOVER ARPEGGIOS	 INTERVALS
 FIFTHS	 MAJOR/MINOR

Creative Powers

 EXPLORE	 CREATIVITY
 LISTENING	 EXPERIMENT
 ARTISTRY	 PERFORMANCE
 IMPROVISE	RHYTHM
KNOWLEDGE	 SONGWRITING

Warm Up

If you have ever listened to the radio or watched a movie, you have heard chords and arpeggios. Chords and arpeggios are found in virtually all music, and are made of combinations of notes. With an arpeggio, you play these notes one at a time. For chords, you play them all together.

In this chapter, we will learn and explore arpeggios. You will find that they are not only easy, but fun - and sound GREAT!

So let's not wait... let's arpeggiate!

WHAT IS AN ARPEGGIO?

TRY A RIGHT HAND ARPEGGIO...

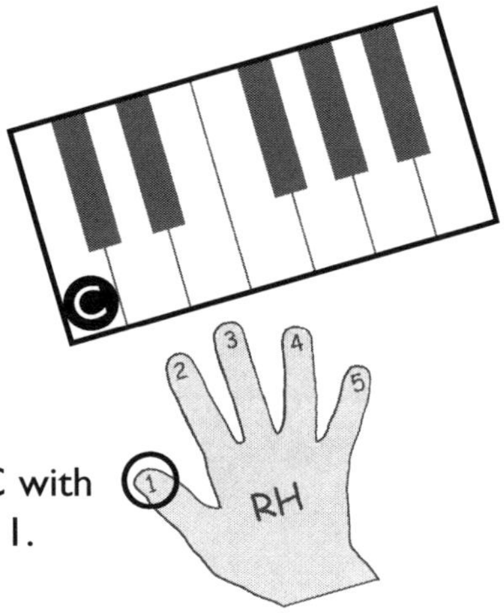

Play C with finger 1.

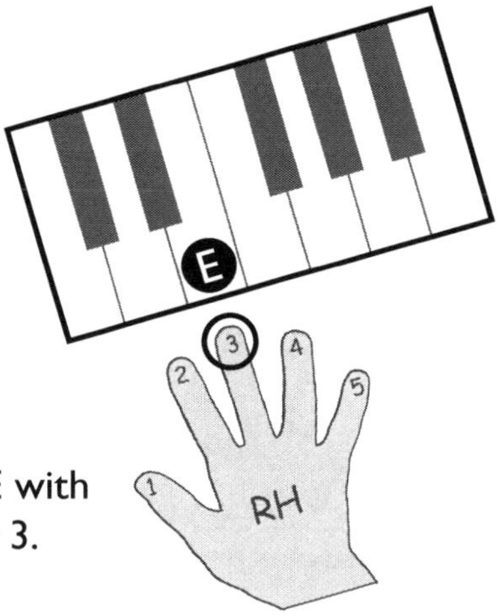

Play E with finger 3.

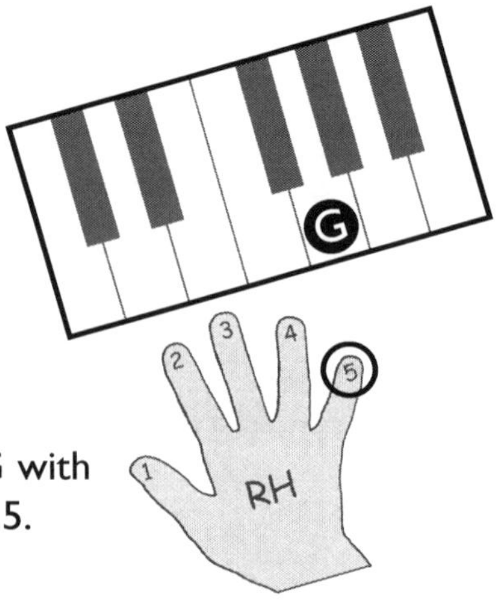

Play G with finger 5.

PRACTICE

Practice right hand arpeggios until they are smooth.
Say/think: "One, two, three" or "Right, two, three."

You don't need to read the music at all. Just play the shapes!

Here is what the pattern looks like on the keyboard.

Root note of the pattern.

Here is what the pattern looks like on the staff.

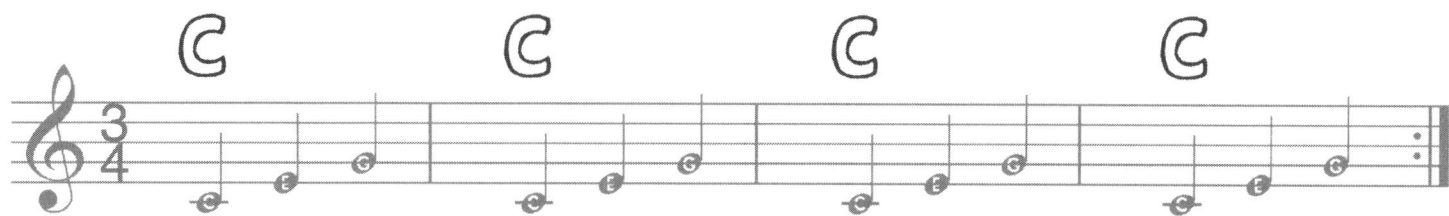

5 SPACE SPIDER (RH) 🕷

Make sure you keep the same hand shape throughout the exercise. Focus on your thumb striking the root note and the rest will fall into place. Say/think: "C, two, three... D, two, three... E, two, three..."

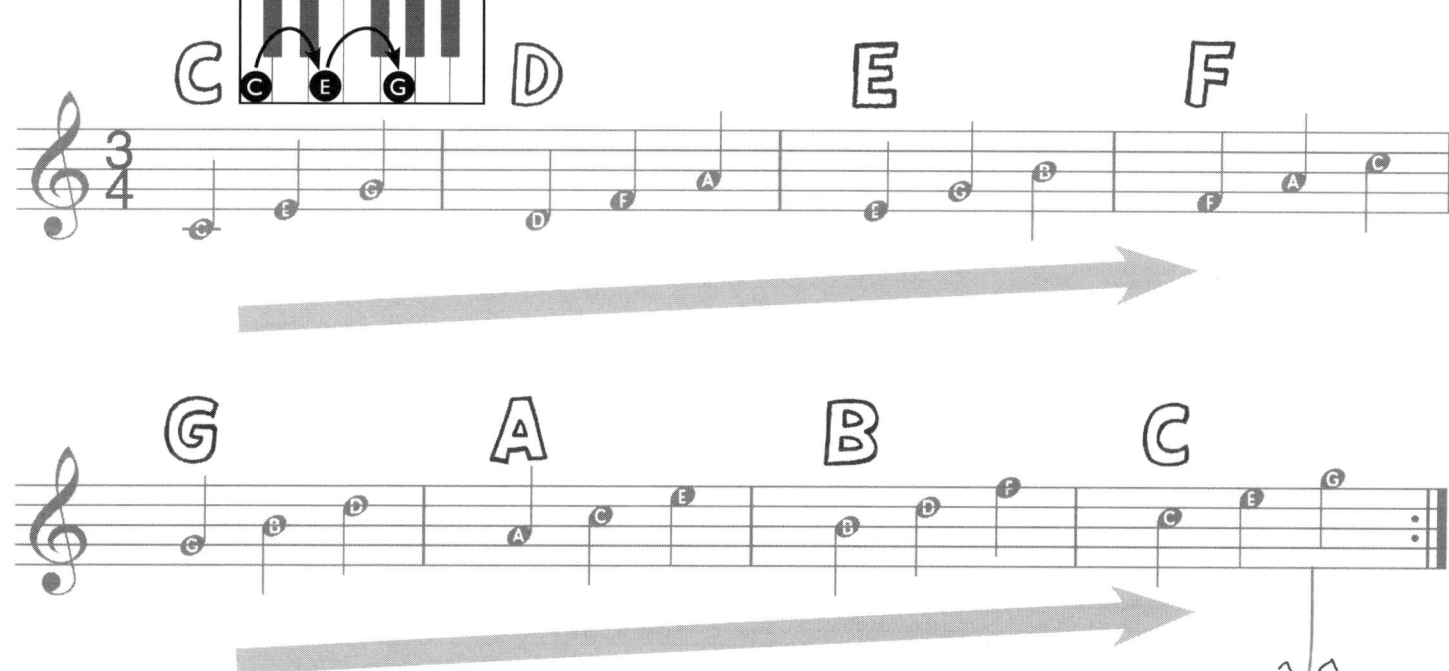

Arpeggios

LEFT HAND ARPEGGIO

Here is a trick to help your hands find their way faster.

Think of your LH pinky (or when it's your right hand, your thumb) as an arrow aiming for a target. The target is the root note (bottom note of the arpeggio)!

If you keep your hand in the correct shape for the pattern, the other fingers will easily find their way.

TRY A LEFT HAND ARPEGGIO...

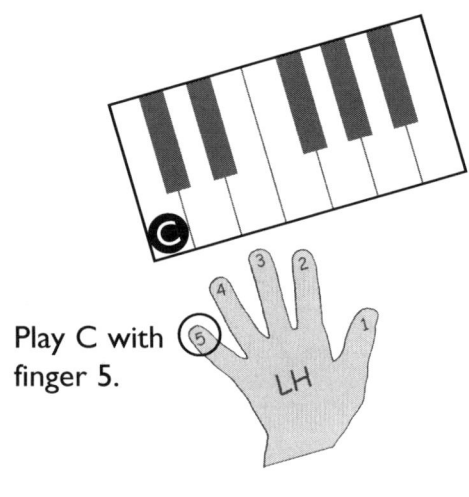

Play C with finger 5.

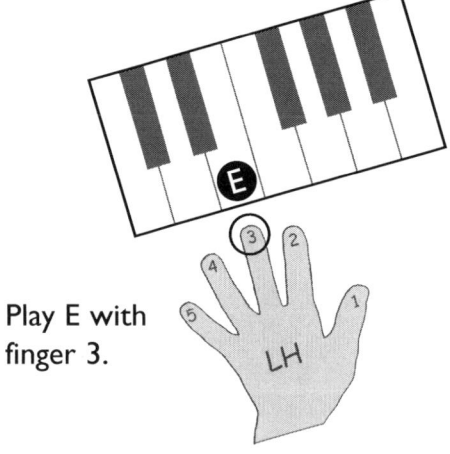

Play E with finger 3.

Use your pinky power!

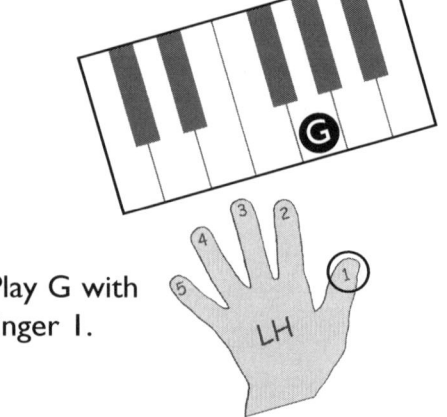

Play G with finger 1.

 SPACE SPIDER (LH) 🕷

Your left hand pinky targets the root note as you climb the arpeggio shape up the keys.
Say/think: "C, two, three... D, two, three... E, two, three..."

CHORD SYMBOLS

The capital letters you see above the staff are called "Chord Symbols." They're named after the root note and help you quickly find what chord or arpeggio you're playing.

Certain types of chords are called "minor" chords. These are noted in the chord symbol, too (like the D minor chord below). There are a few ways to notate this: Dmin, Dm, or even with a minus sign: D-

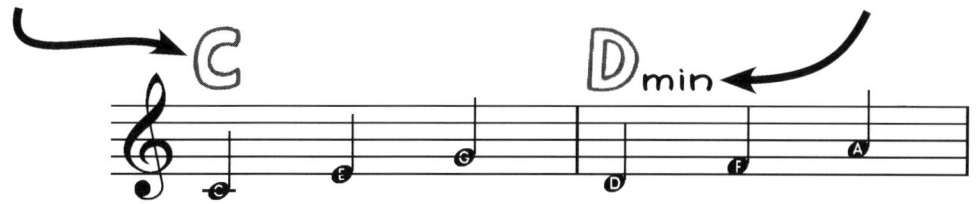

You'll learn more about minor (and major) chords in Chapter 8.

ROOT TRICK

Think of a plant with a root at the bottom. The other notes in the chord are flowers!

Arpeggios

TWO-HANDED ARPEGGIOS

PLACE HANDS...

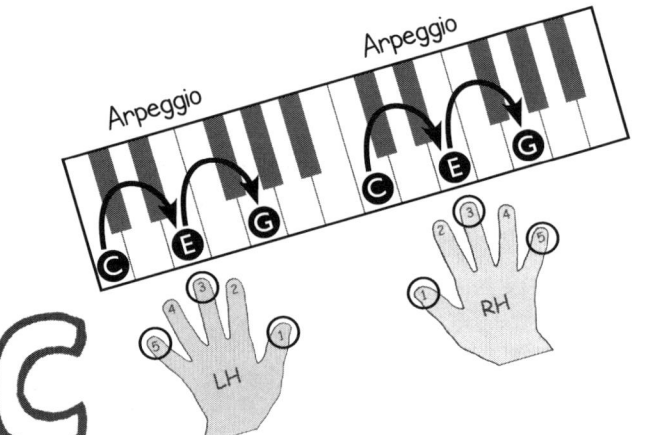

- Place your left hand pinky on bass C and your right hand thumb on middle C. This position is called C position.
- Play a C arpeggio with your left hand.
- Answer with a C arpeggio in your right hand.
- Move both hands up to D position, repeat the pattern, and keep going...

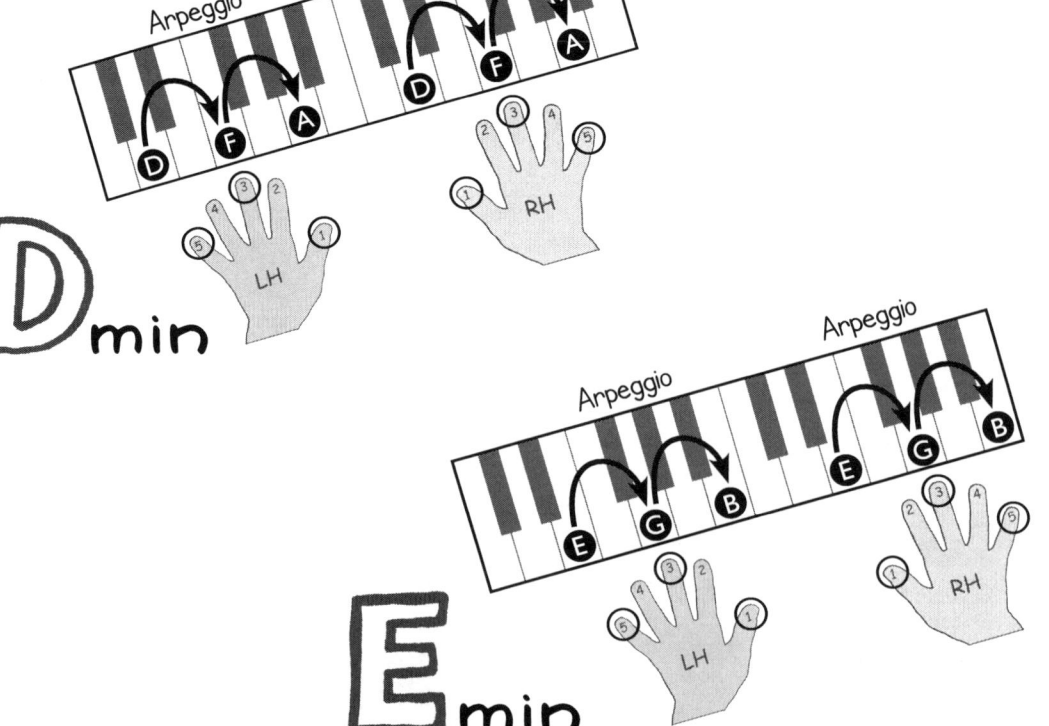

 ASTRONOMICAL ARPEGGIOS

Say/think: "Left, two, three. Right, two three..."

*There is another less common type of chord known as a diminished chord. Look it up!

LISTEN!

Now that you know about arpeggios, you'll start to hear them everywhere. Your mission: Find and listen to some iconic arpeggio songs.

<u>Some suggestions:</u>   Moonlight Sonata   Unchained Melody
House of the Rising Sun   And thousands more!

COMPLETE! ☐

LISTENING

Arpeggios

WHAT IS A CHORD PROGRESSION?

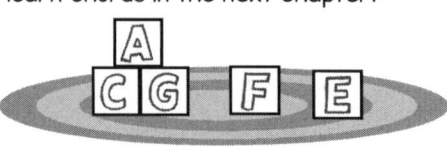

8. MAGNETIC MALAGUENA

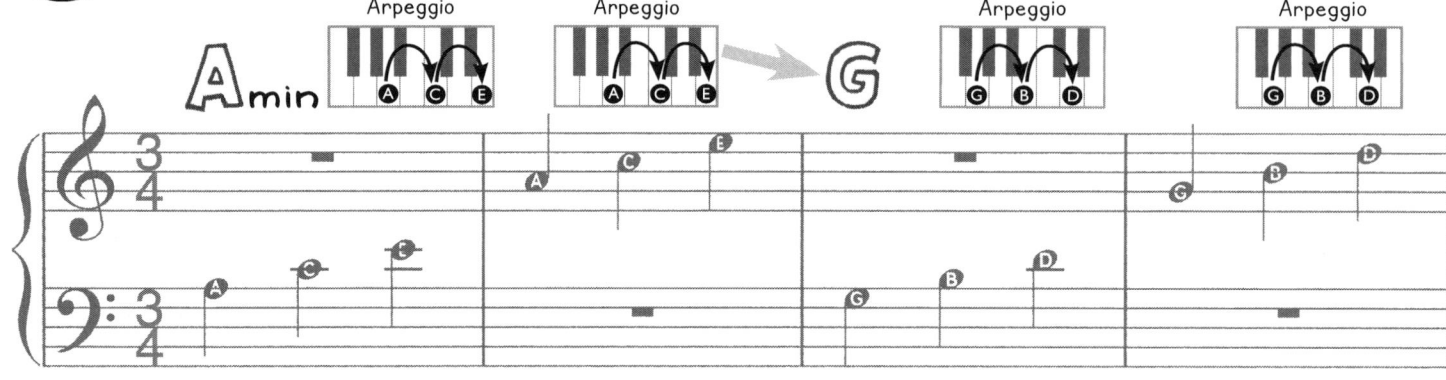
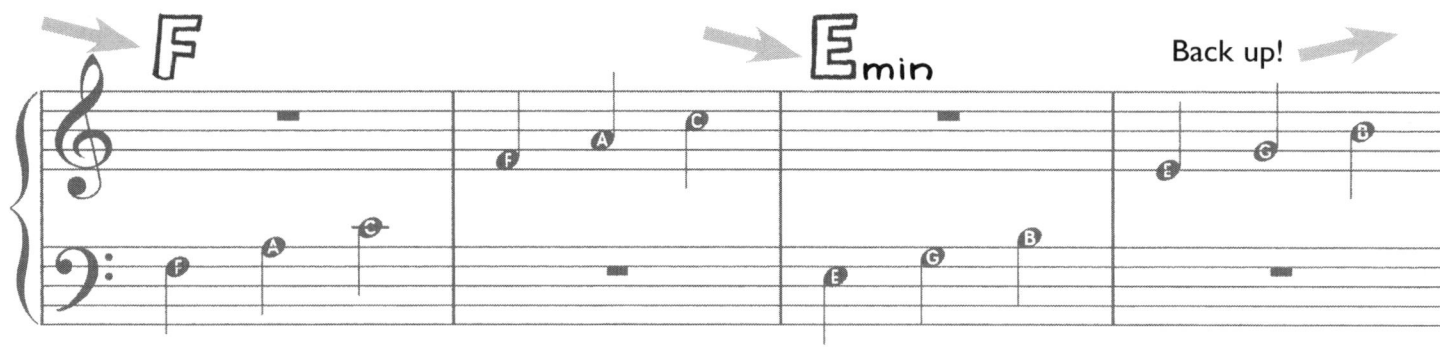
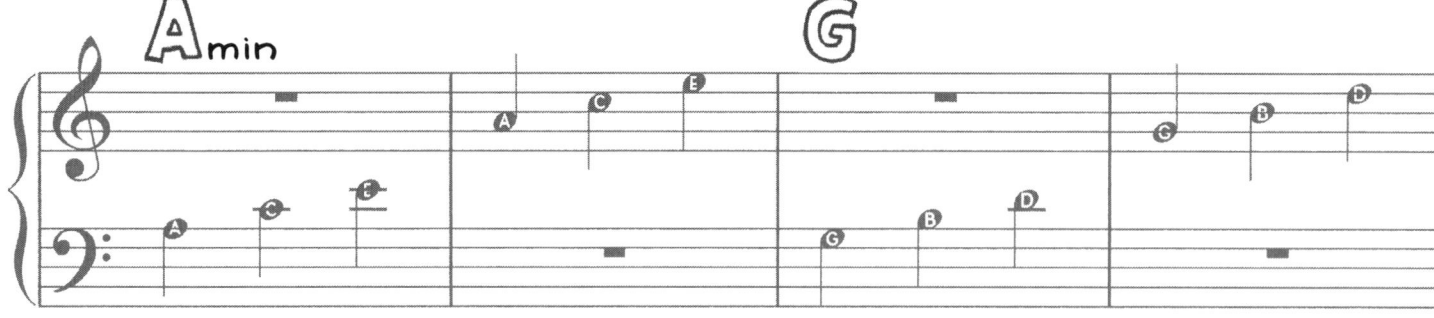
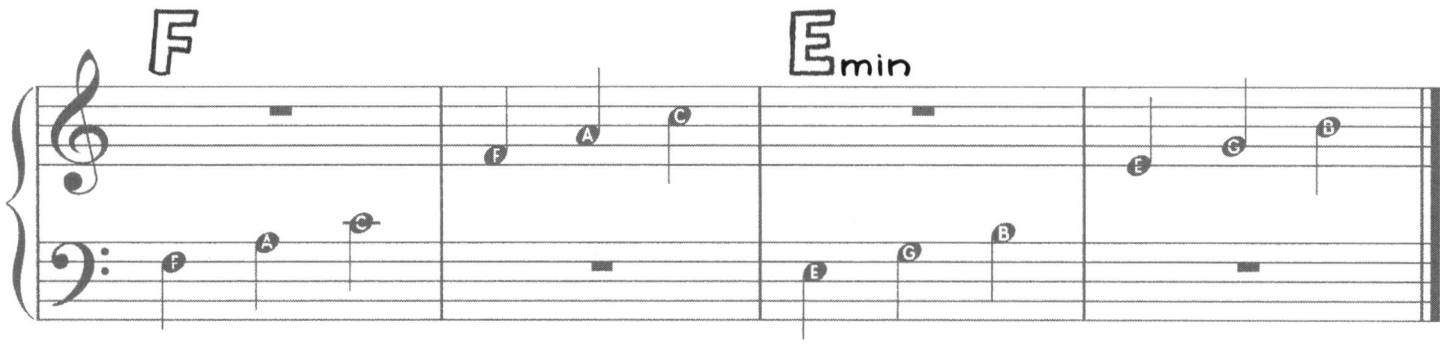

Arpeggios

CELESTIAL BALLAD

Can you hear/feel the difference between this ballad progression and the Malaguena?

This progression was used in the song "Time After Time." Look it up! Can you sing it?

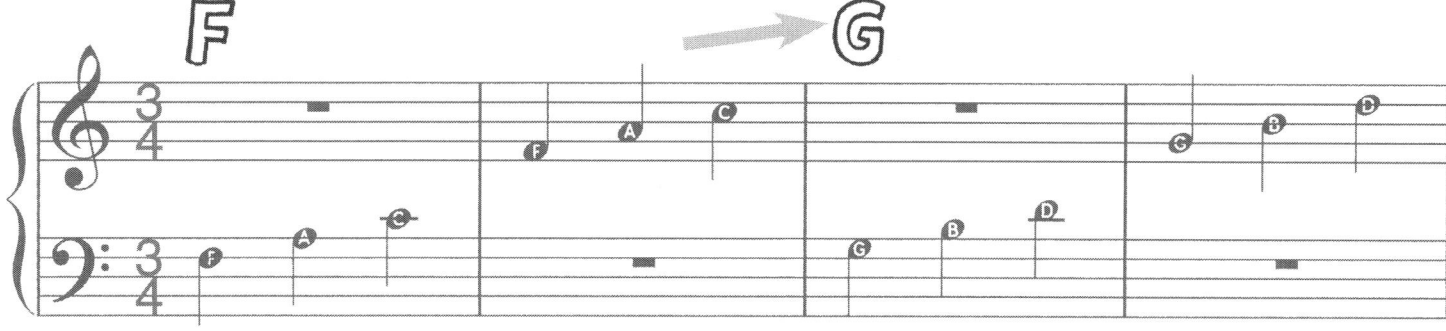

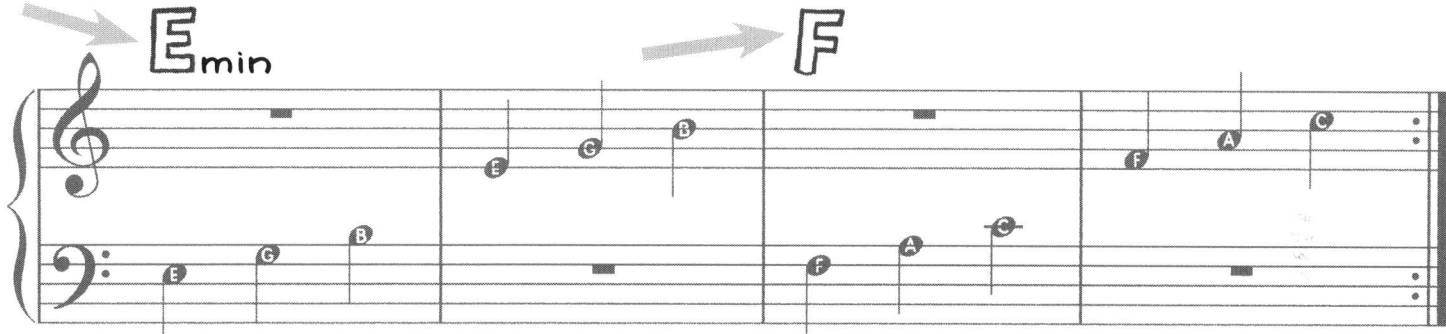

...And this one has been used tons of times - from songs like "Jack and Diane" to the theme from "Titanic."

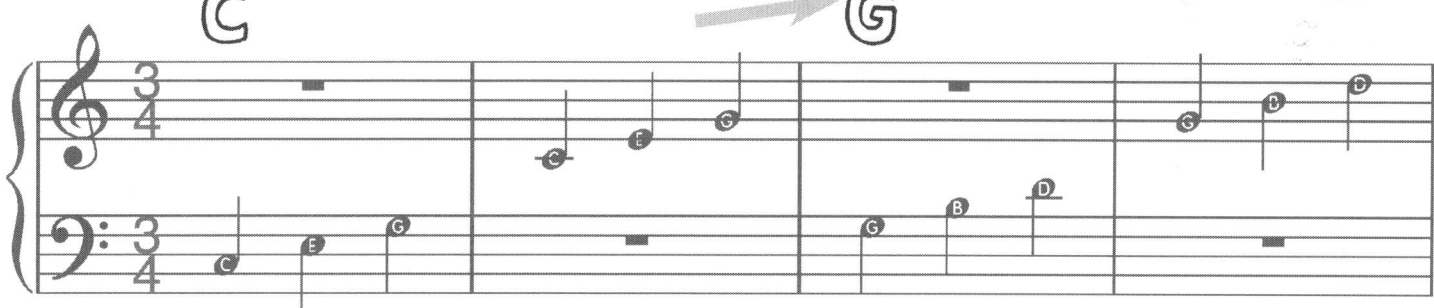

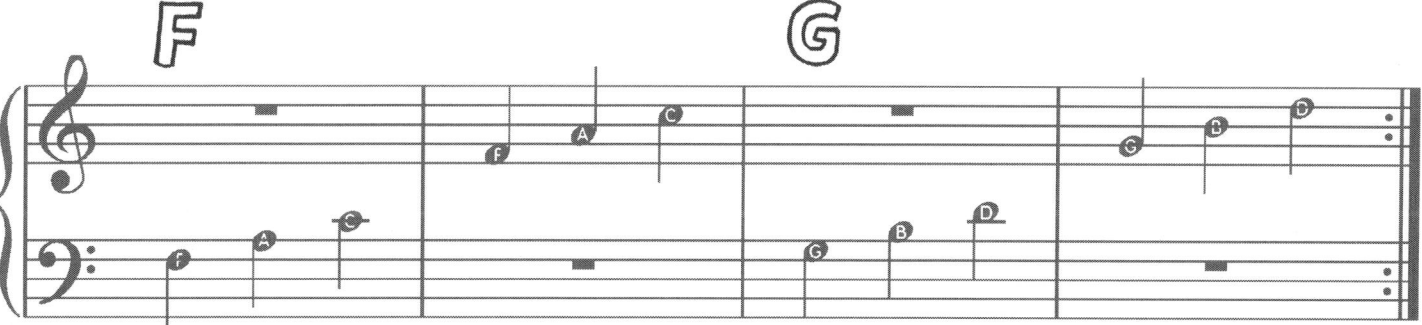

Try playing this piece and others with the games in a Meridee Winters Game Book!

Arpeggios

Get into the FLOW

ARPEGGIOS UP AND DOWN

In this exercise, your hands will move like waves up and down the keyboard. Tip: to get into the flow, sway your body like waves as you play!

PLACE YOUR HANDS...

- Starting on C, play two-handed arpeggios as you have been.
- Keep your hands in the same position.
- Start with the top note (RH pinky) and play the same notes you just played in the opposite direction - from the top note to the bottom note.
- Practice this until you can play it smoothly.

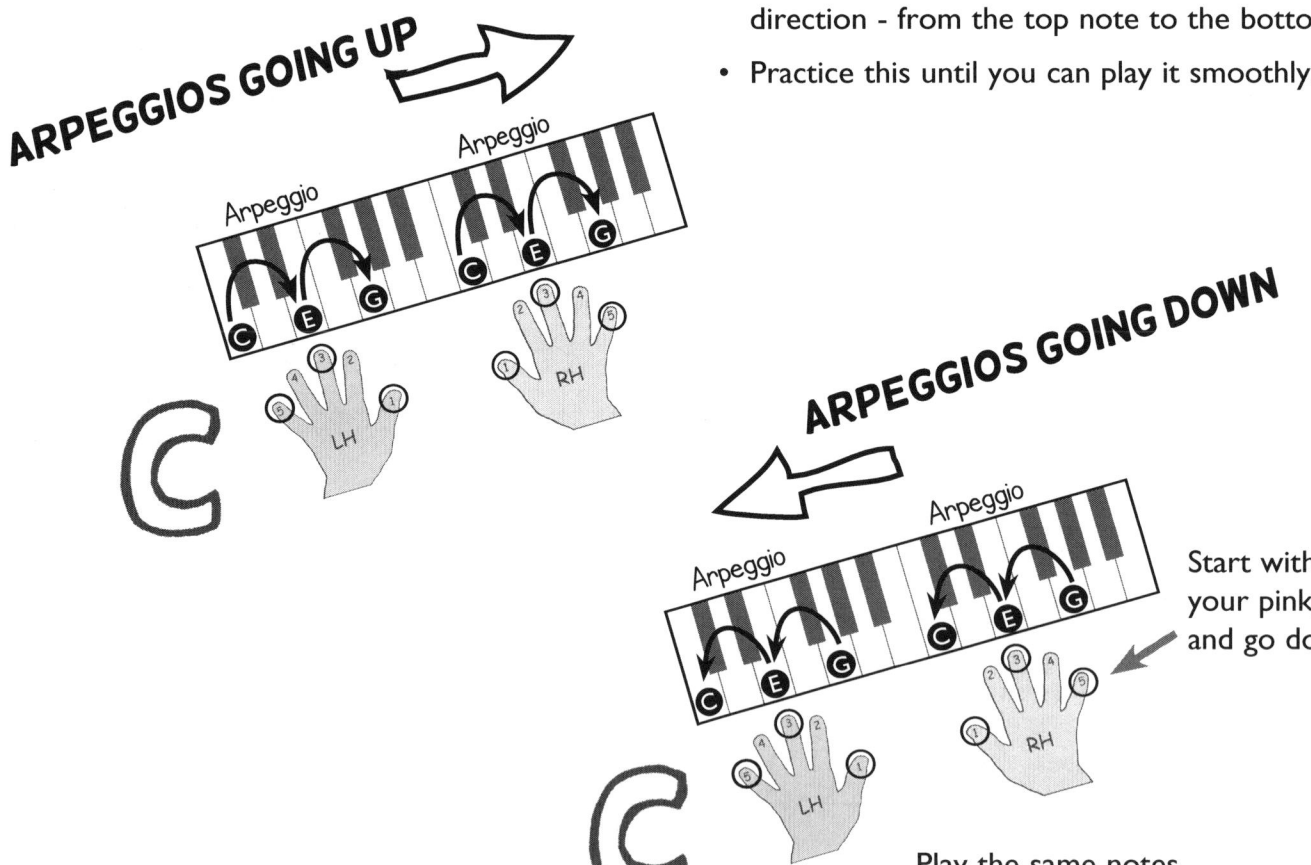

Start with your pinky and go down.

Play the same notes as before but in the opposite direction.

11 WAVES

Say/Think: "Left, two, three... Right, two, three... DOWN, two three... DOWN, two, three...".

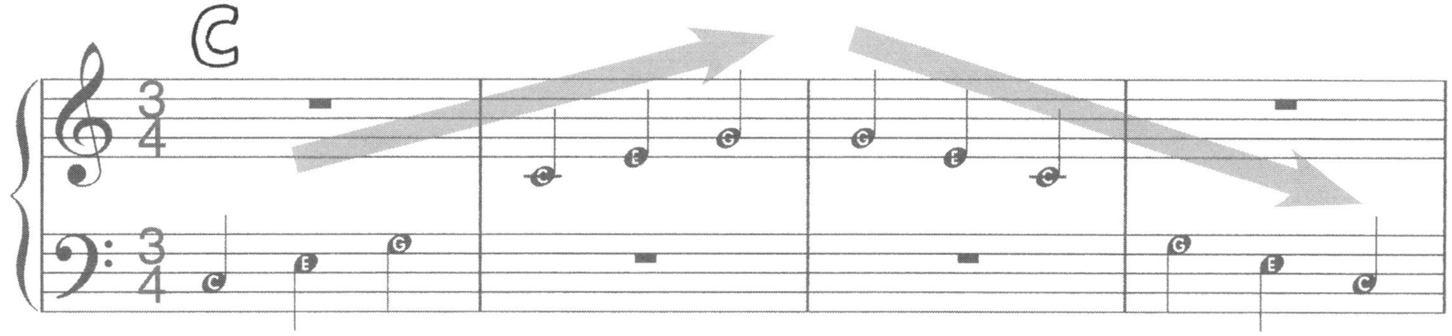

C

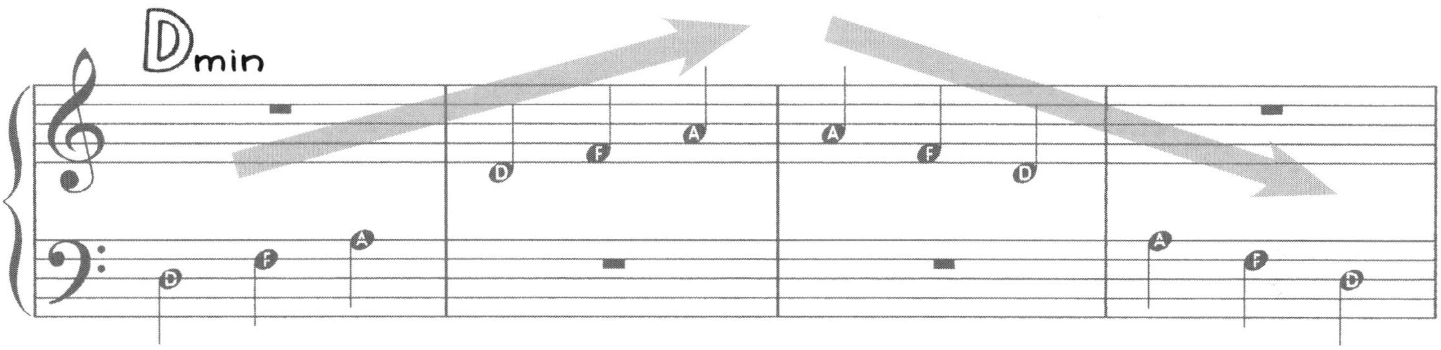

Dmin

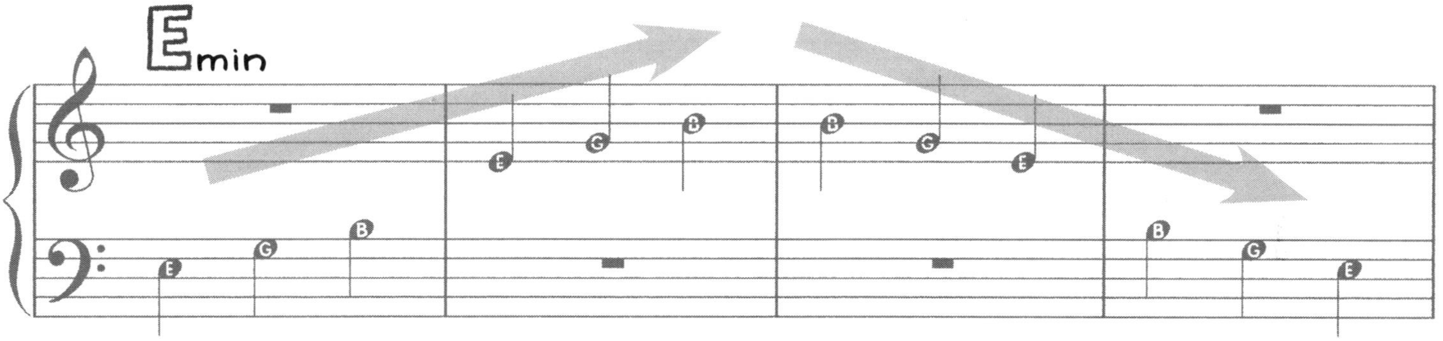

Emin

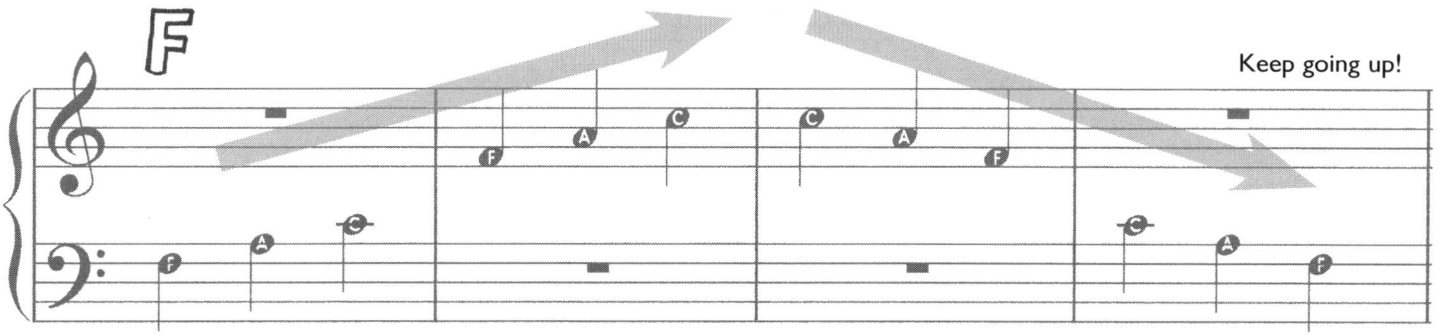

F

Keep going up!

CHALLENGE!

Try playing the pattern in the following ways:

- Play high or low waves.
- Play soft or loud waves.
- Try it with the metronome.

Arpeggios

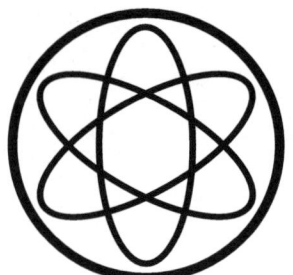# QUANTUM QUIZ!

 1 KNOWLEDGE:

WHAT IS A CHORD PROGRESSION?
_____
_____

 2 PLAY

PLAY AN APREGGIO (RIGHT HAND, THEN LEFT) STARTING ON THESE ROOT NOTES:

 CREATE!

COMBINE THE ARPEGGIOS IN STEP 2 IN ANY ORDER TO MAKE YOUR OWN SONG!

My Progression:

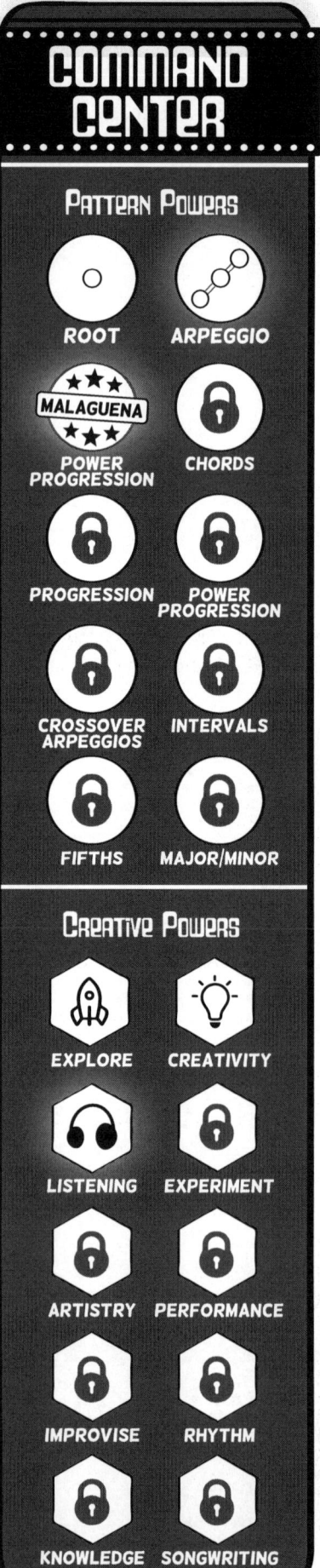

Arpeggios

Once you can play chords and arpeggios, a whole universe of music is open to you! You can learn progressions to famous songs, play in bands, write your own music and so much more.

Since you already know arpeggios, chords will be a breeze! Just play the same notes, but all at the same time. Like last chapter, we'll practice playing the shape, then make amazing music.

Let's play!

WHAT IS A CHORD?

STEP 1 TRY IT...

ARPEGGIO

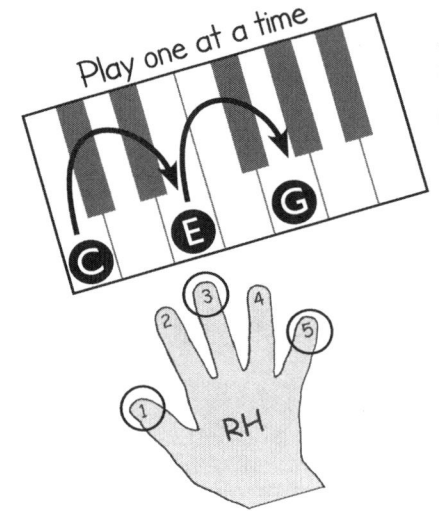

An arpeggio is played one note at a time.

CHORD

Chords are those same notes played all at once.

Get it? Chords and arpeggios are the same thing, just played differently. An arpeggio is often called a broken chord.

 # STEP 2: LOOK AT THE SHAPE ON THE KEYBOARD AND STAFF

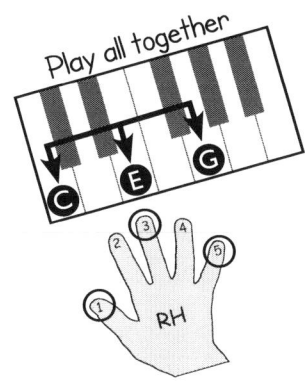 = 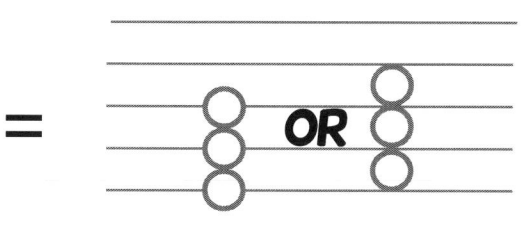 OR

Chords on the staff look like snowmen!

Notes of the chord are stacked one above the other on the staff — which means you play them all at once. The basic chords we play in this book are either line-line-line or space-space-space.

 # STEP 3: PRACTICE...

Play chords with each hand separately until you are comfortable.

 **RH**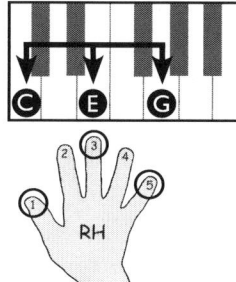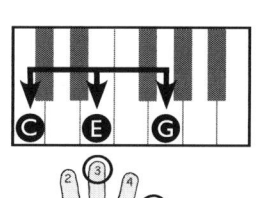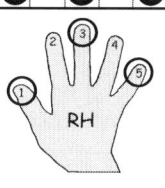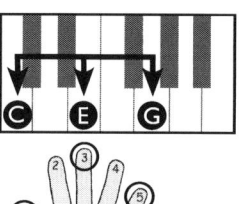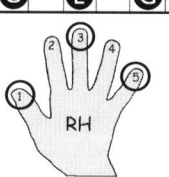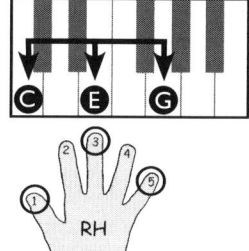

 **LH**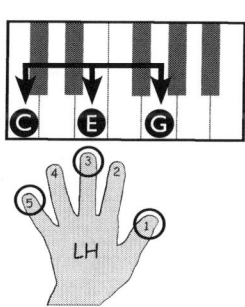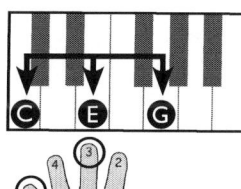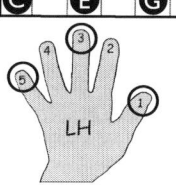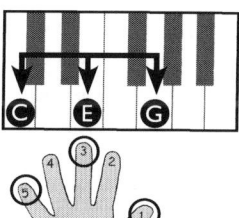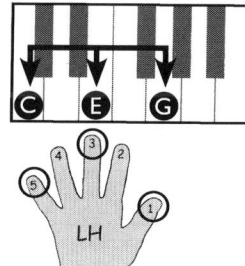

Chords

12 CHORD SCALE CLIMB

Climb up the scale using arpeggios and chords. Say/think: "Arpeggio, arpeggio, chord, chord."

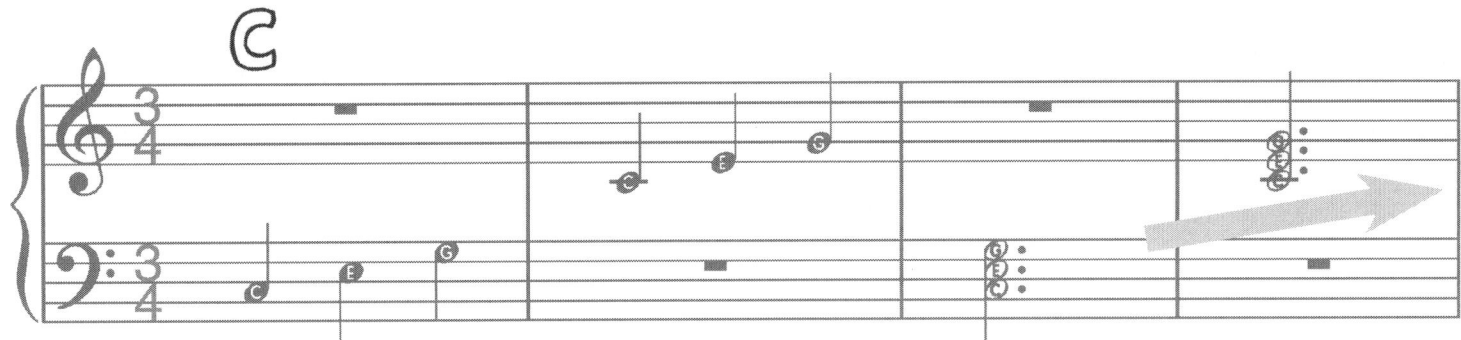

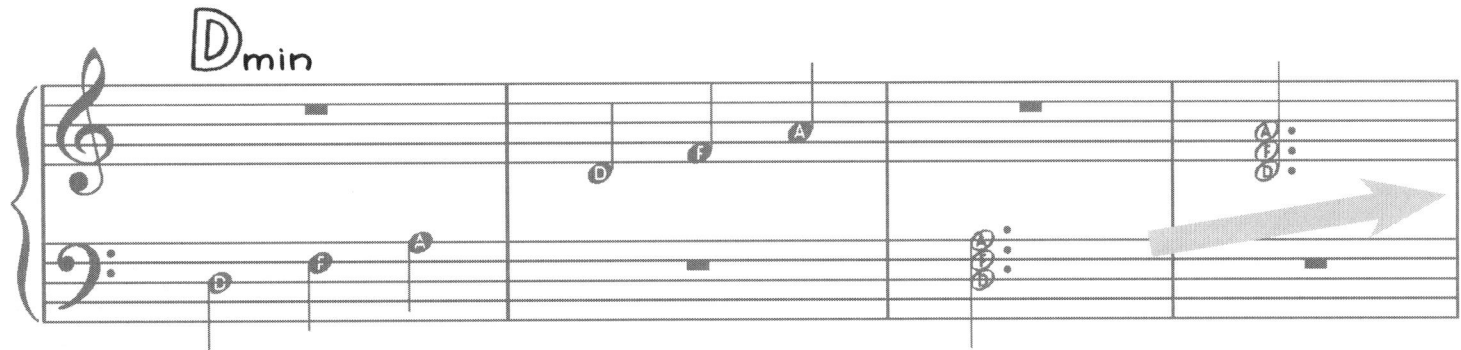

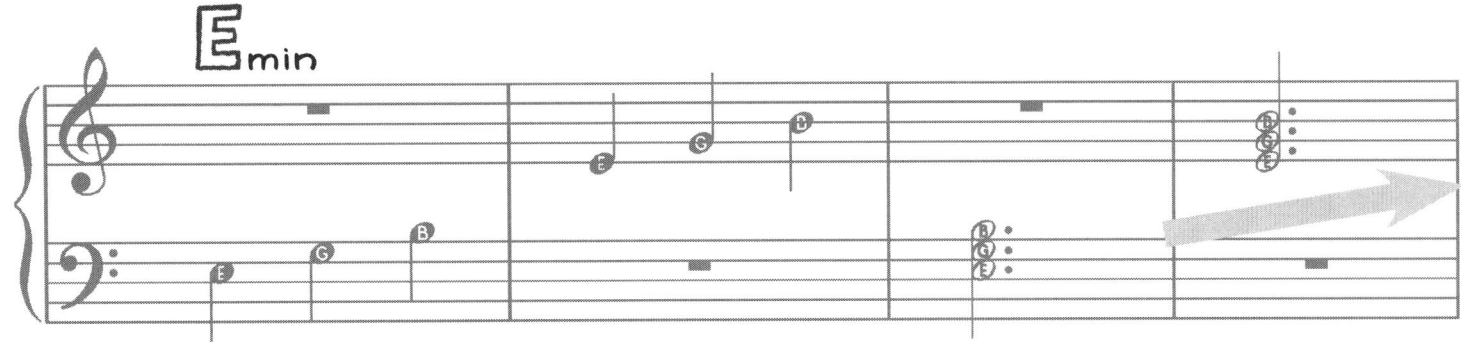

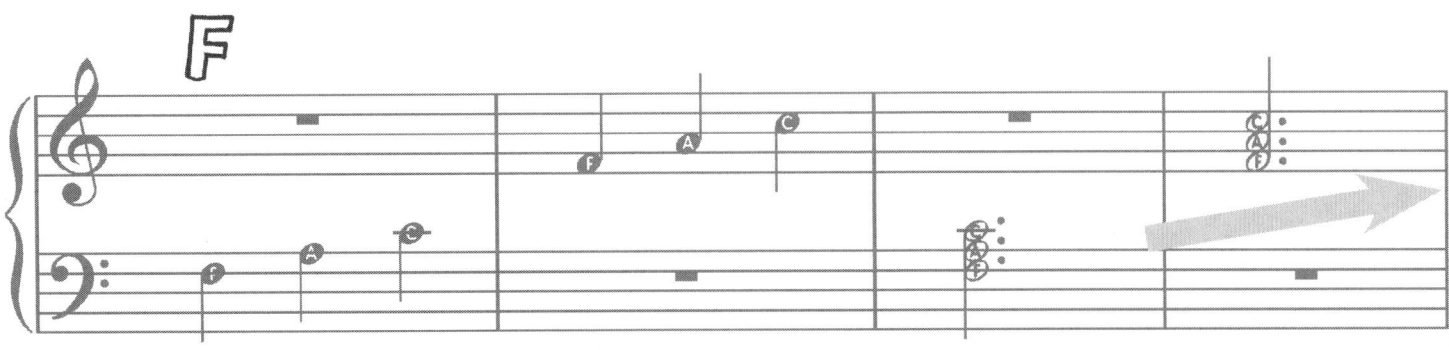

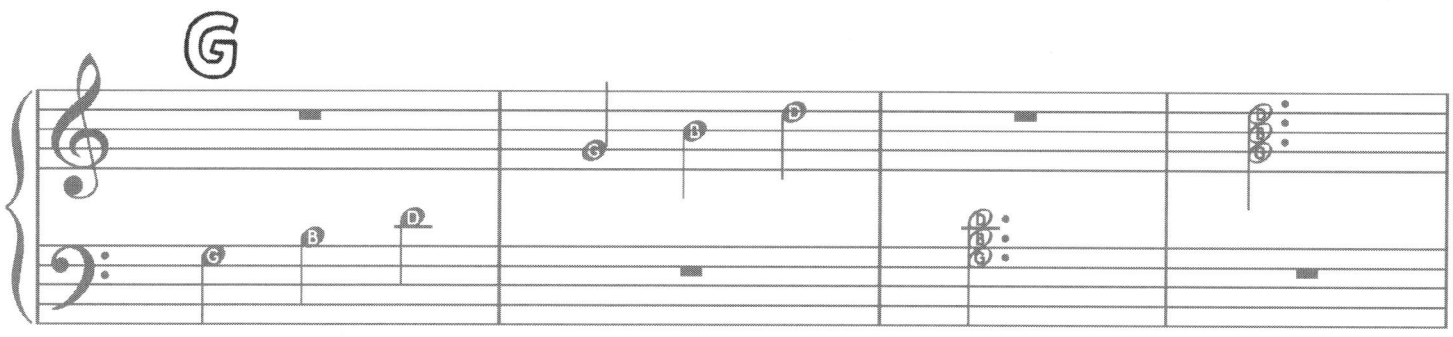

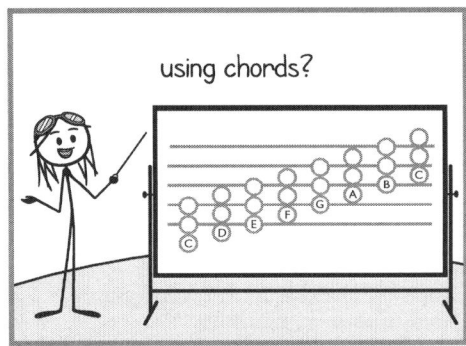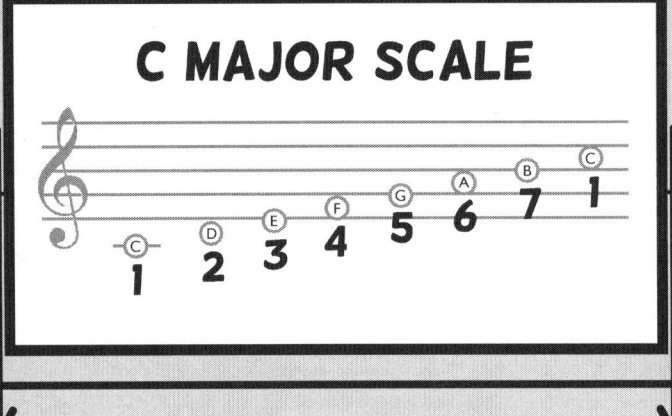

13 CHORD SCALE SUMMIT

Now say it and play it!

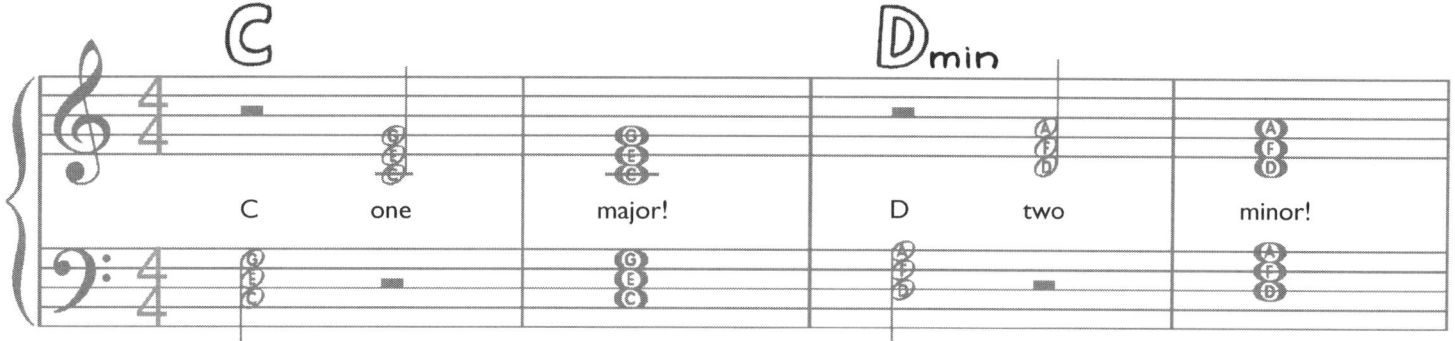

Chords

37

14 CHORD CONSTELLATION

Now try this chord pattern with a rock progression!

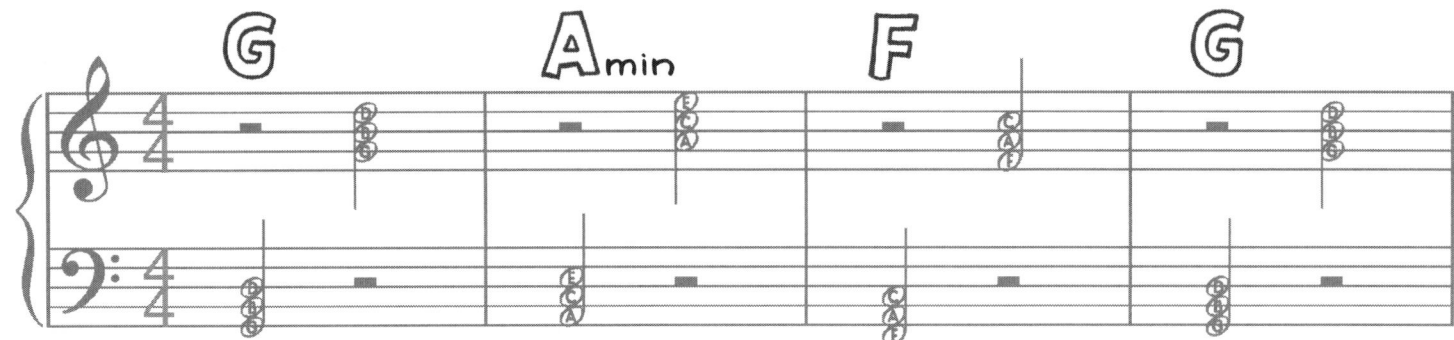

Try all of these exercises with a metronome!

15 ROCK-ET CHORDS

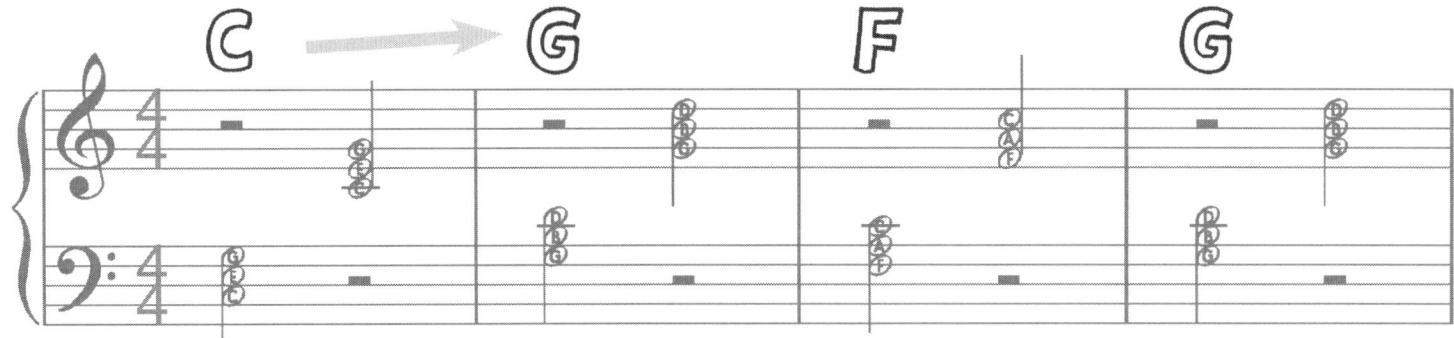

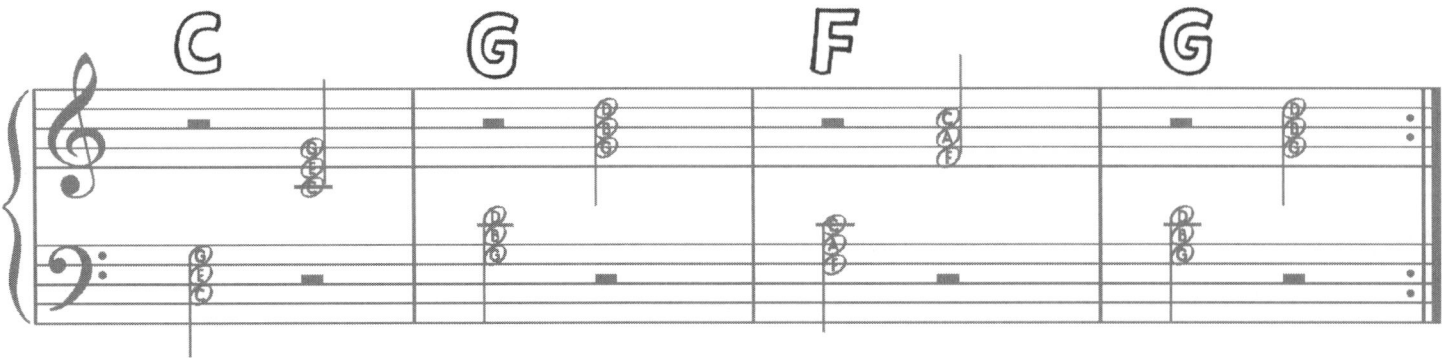

16 MALAGUENA CHORD COMBINATION 1

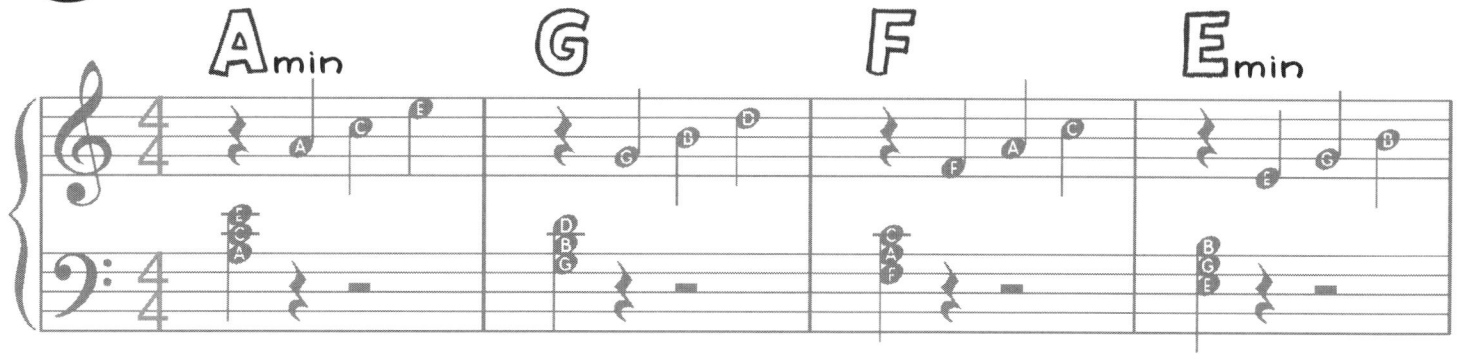

Try it as a duet! One person can play the excercise while the other improvises.

17 MALAGUENA CHORD COMBINATION 2

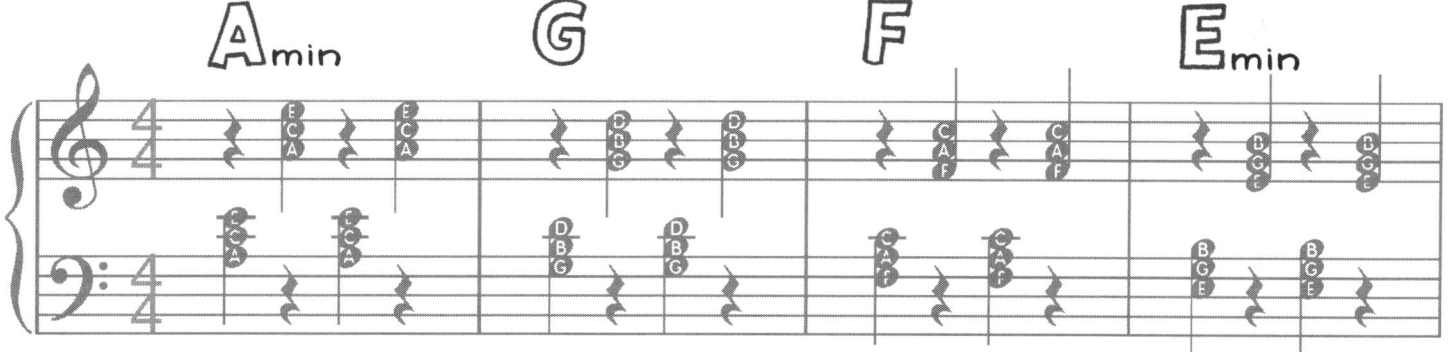

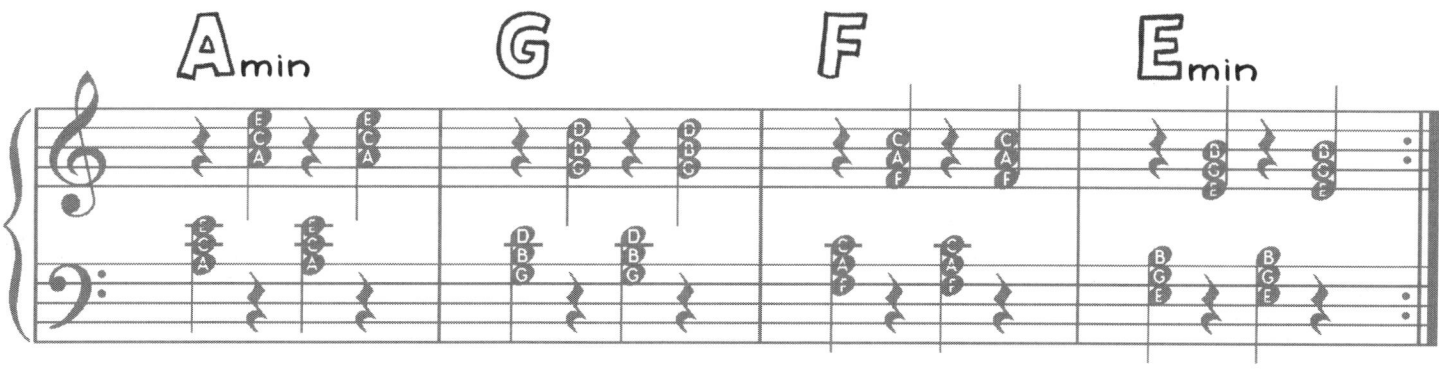

DEEP SPACE DOO WOP

DOO WOP PATTERN 1

Play this pattern with DOO WOP Pattern 1. Move your hands to each new postion and repeat the pattern as you go.

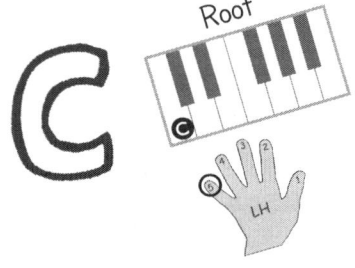
First play the root note (C) once with your LH finger 5.

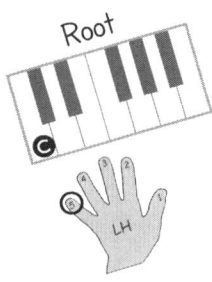
Repeat the root note.

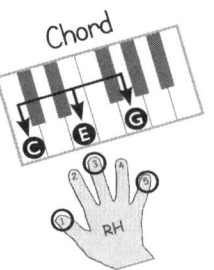
With your RH in C position, play a C chord.

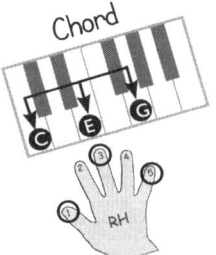
Repeat the chord.

DOO WOP PATTERN 2

Play this pattern with DOO WOP Pattern 2. As the chords change, move your hands to each new postion and repeat the pattern.

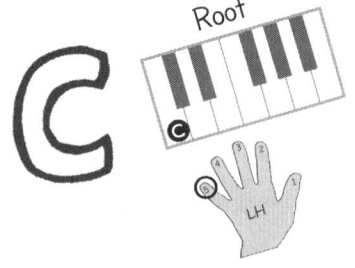
Play the root note (C) once with your LH finger 5.

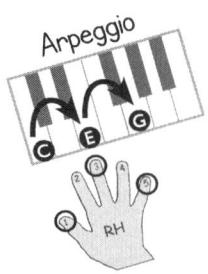
With your RH in C position, play a C arpeggio.

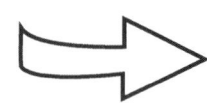

18 DOO WOP PATTERN 1

Now play the entire pattern/progression together. Say/think:
"Left, left, right, right" or "Root, root, chord, chord."

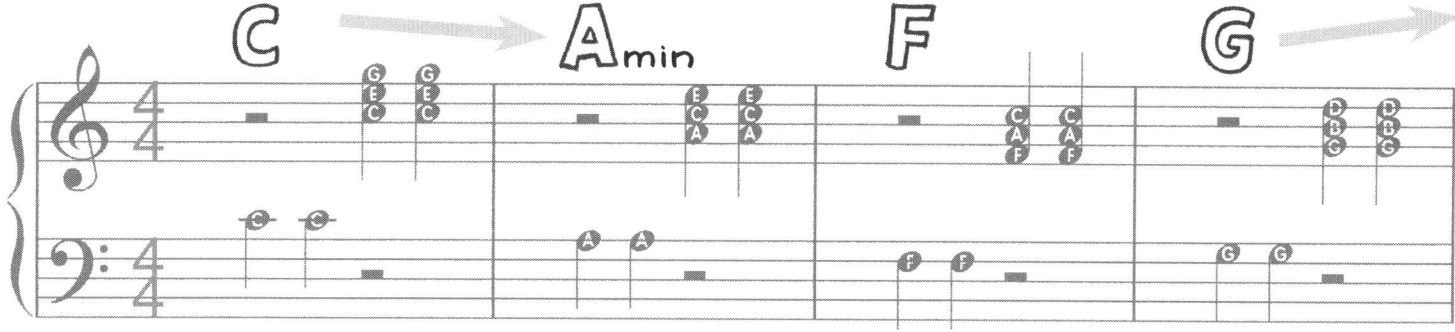

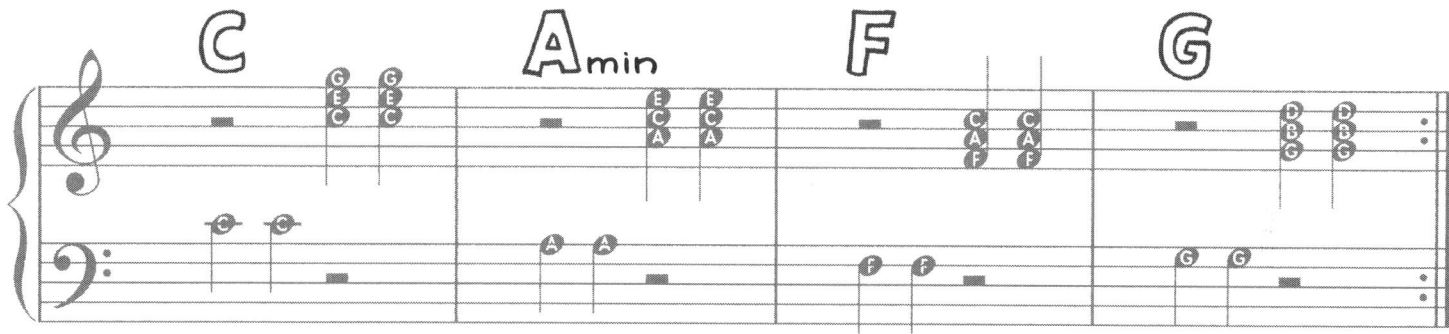

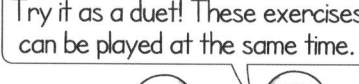

19 DOO WOP PATTERN 2

Now play Doo Wop Pattern 2 with the progression.
Say/think: "Left, two, three, four."

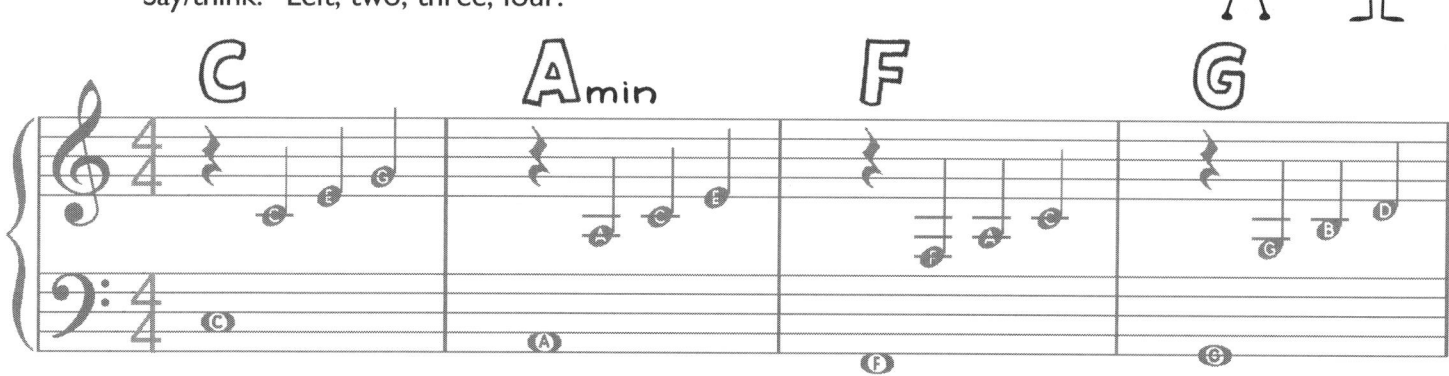

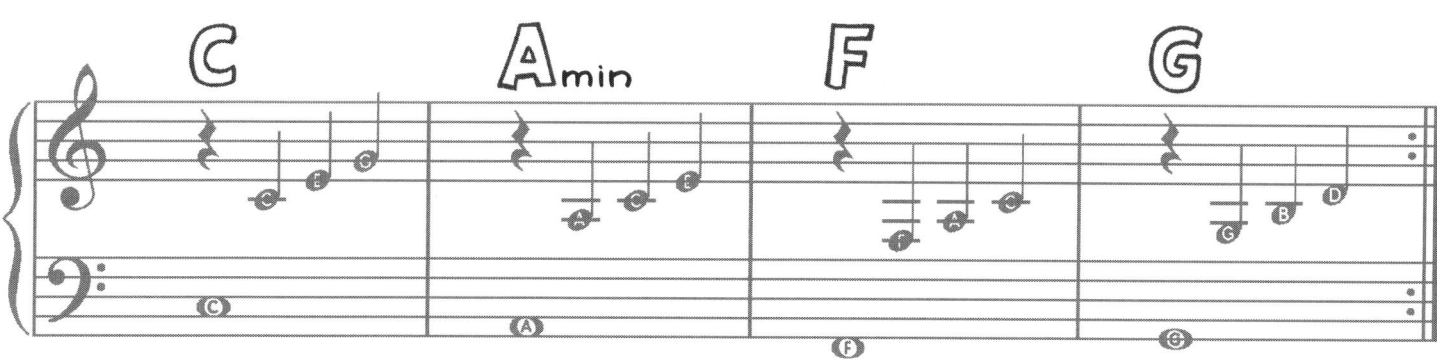

Chords

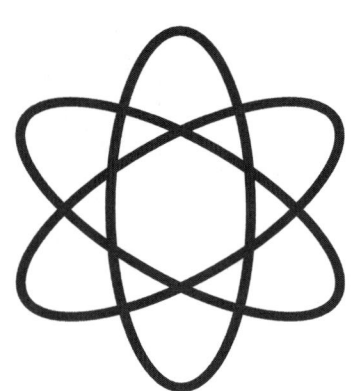

LET'S EXPERIMENT!

We'll combine chords to build our progressions!

STEP 1 CHOOSE FROM THESE CHORDS

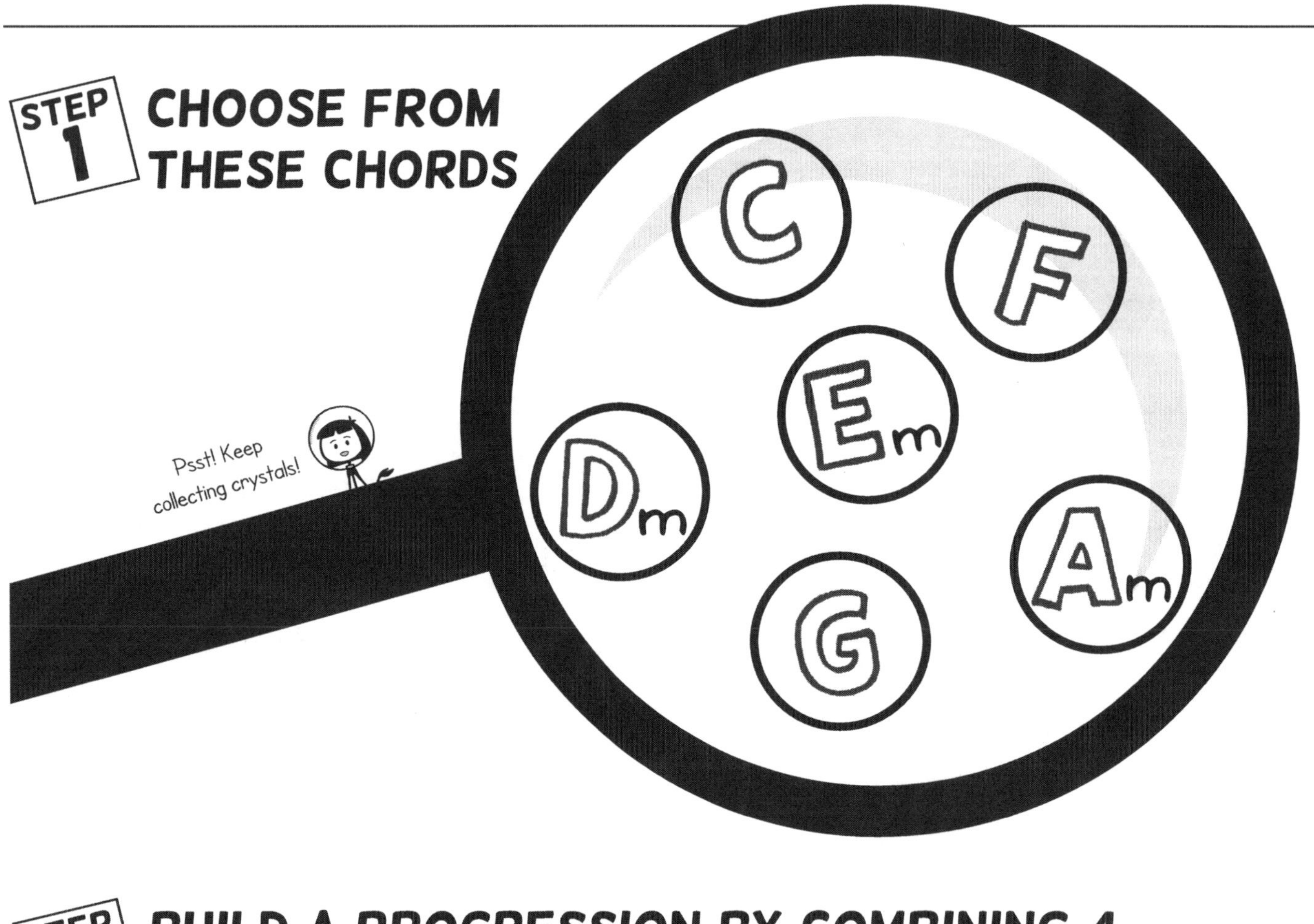

C, F, Em, Dm, G, Am

Psst! Keep collecting crystals!

STEP 2 BUILD A PROGRESSION BY COMBINING 4 CHORDS FROM ABOVE LIKE OUR EXAMPLE:

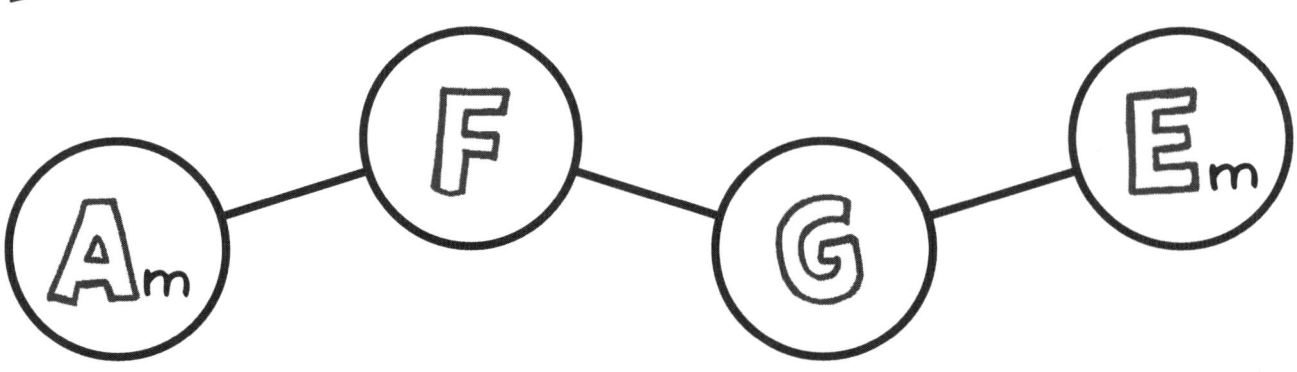

Am — F — G — Em

Chords

STEP 3: SEE YOUR RESULTS!

Play and experiment until you find progressions you like!

EXPERIMENT

PROGRESSION 1:

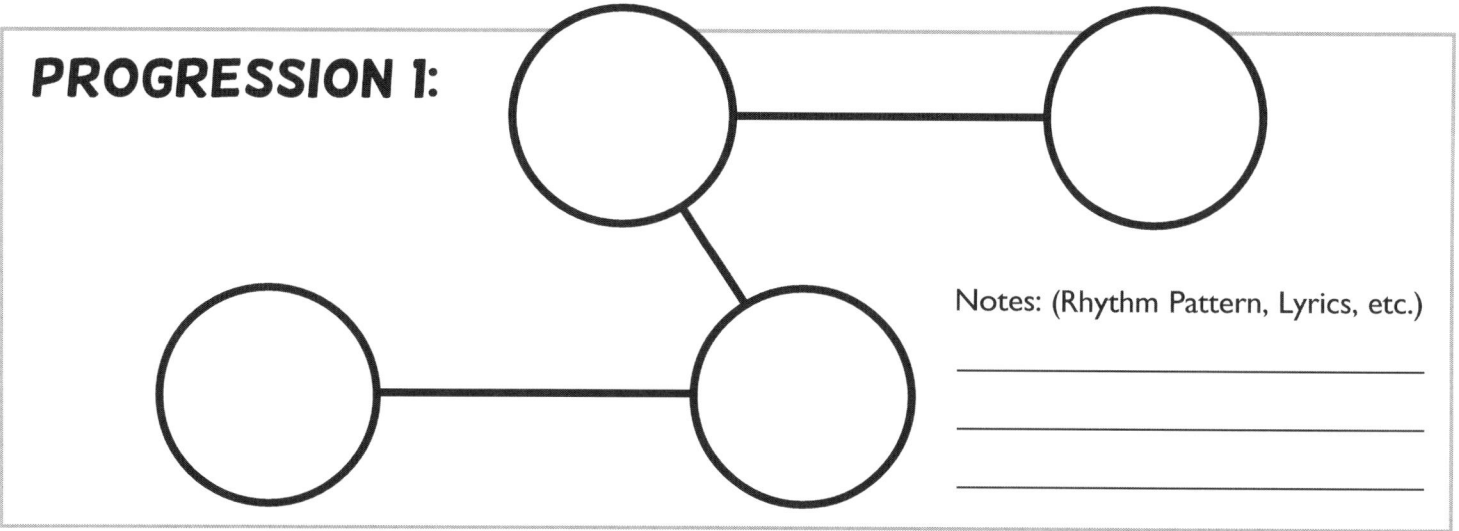

Notes: (Rhythm Pattern, Lyrics, etc.)
_____
_____
_____

PROGRESSION 2:

Notes: _____
_____
_____

PROGRESSION 3:

Notes: _____
_____
_____

Tip! Progressions don't always have to contain 4 chords. It's common to have progressions with 8 or 12 chords, too. See if you can come up with a longer progression!

QUANTUM QUIZ!

1. KNOWLEDGE:
WITH AN ARPEGGIO, YOU PLAY _____ AT A TIME.
WITH A CHORD, YOU PLAY THE NOTES _____.

2. PLAY
PLAY A CHORD WITH YOUR RIGHT HAND, THEN LEFT, STARTING ON THESE ROOT NOTES:

G — COMPLETE! ☐   F — COMPLETE! ☐   C — COMPLETE! ☐

3. PLAY
THE MALAGUENA PROGRESSION, USING CHORDS, FROM MEMORY.   COMPLETE! ☐

Amazing! You've earned your Chord, Progression and Experiment powers!

Chords were fun!

Now let's learn something famous!

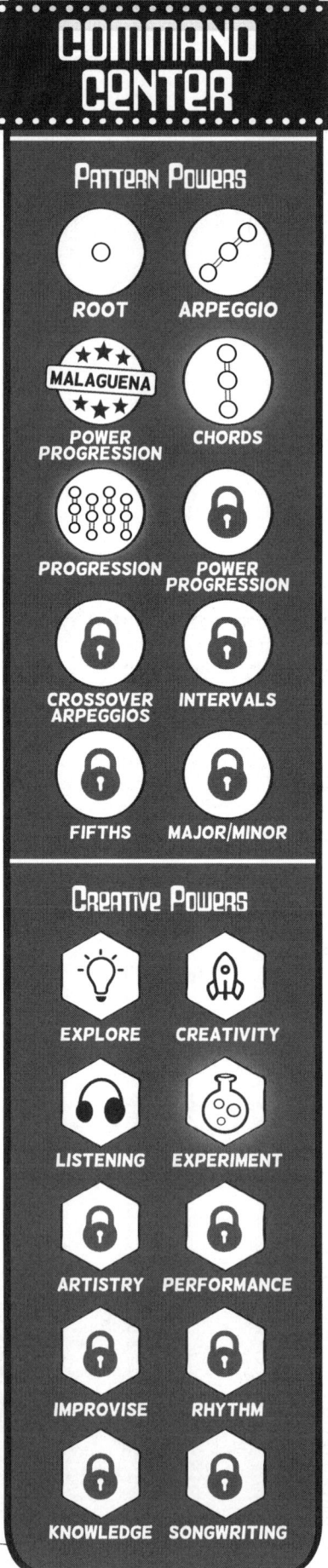

COMMAND CENTER

Pattern Powers
- ROOT
- ARPEGGIO
- MALAGUENA — POWER PROGRESSION
- CHORDS
- PROGRESSION
- POWER PROGRESSION 🔒
- CROSSOVER ARPEGGIOS 🔒
- INTERVALS 🔒
- FIFTHS 🔒
- MAJOR/MINOR 🔒

Creative Powers
- EXPLORE
- CREATIVITY
- LISTENING
- EXPERIMENT
- ARTISTRY 🔒
- PERFORMANCE 🔒
- IMPROVISE 🔒
- RHYTHM 🔒
- KNOWLEDGE 🔒
- SONGWRITING 🔒

CHAPTER 4
CHORD CONCERT: PACHELBEL

Now that you know chords, arpeggios and chord progressions, you can perform your own amazing concert!

Composed over 300 years ago in 1680, Pachelbel's Canon has never gone out of style, making it one of the most popular classical compositions of all time. It has been performed thousands of times by artists from all different genres of music – from chamber groups to rock bands, orchestras to punk, and now... by YOU!

Chord Concert: Pachelbel

PACHELBEL'S CANON

THE PROGRESSION: C G A min E min F C F G

This progression is famous. Let's perform it a few different ways!

🔟 PATTERN 1: ARPEGGIO, ARPEGGIO

21 PATTERN 2: ROOT, ARPEGGIO

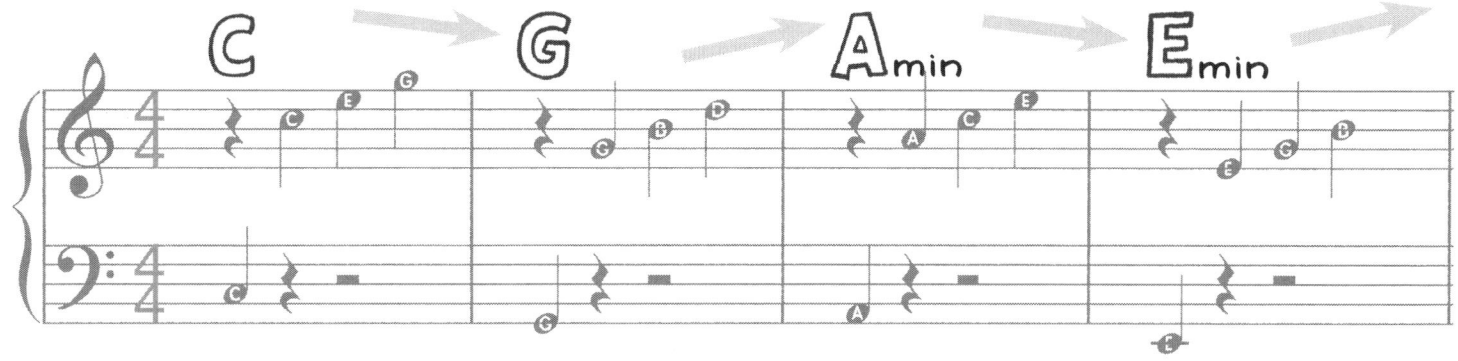

22 PATTERN 3: ARPEGGIO, CHORD

Got it down? Perform it for a friend or family member!

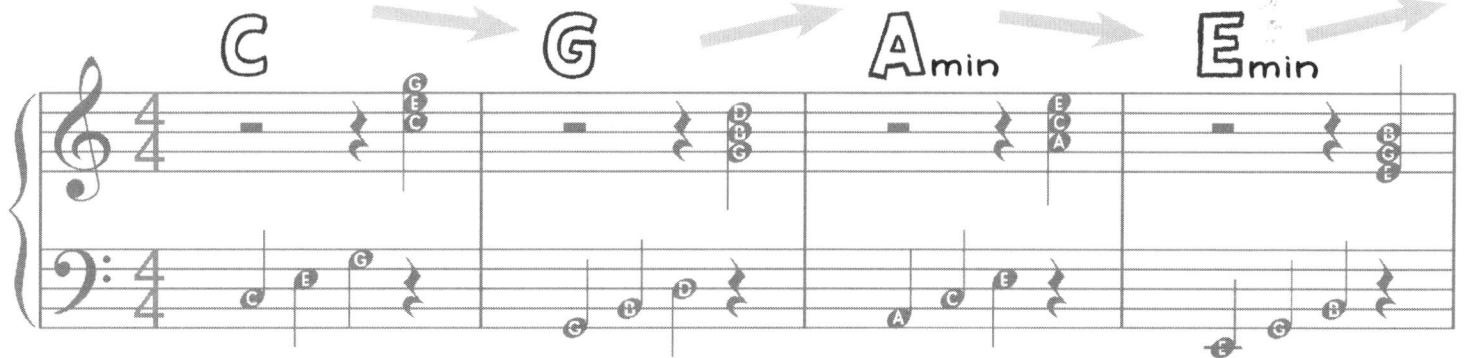

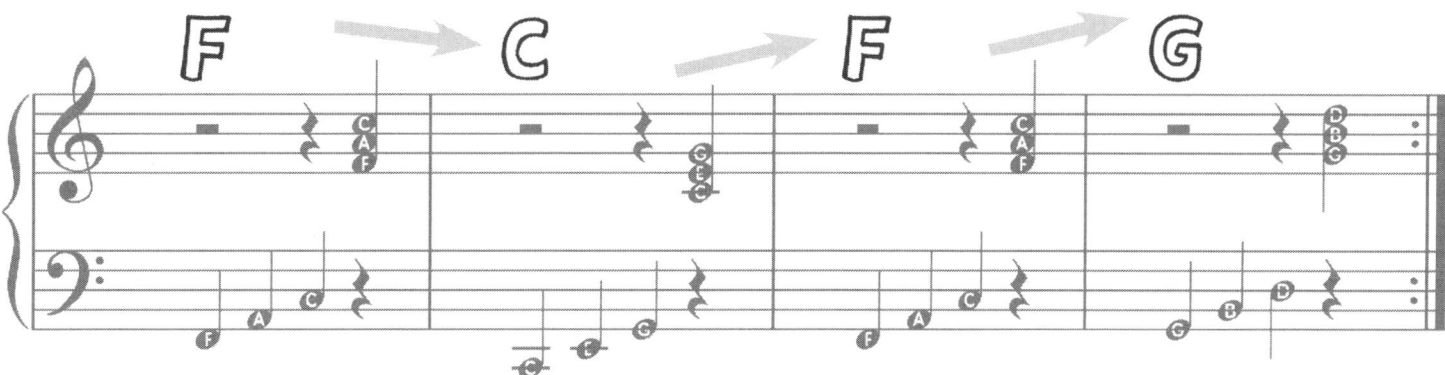

Chord Concert: Pachelbel

23 PATTERN 4: CHORD, ARPEGGIO

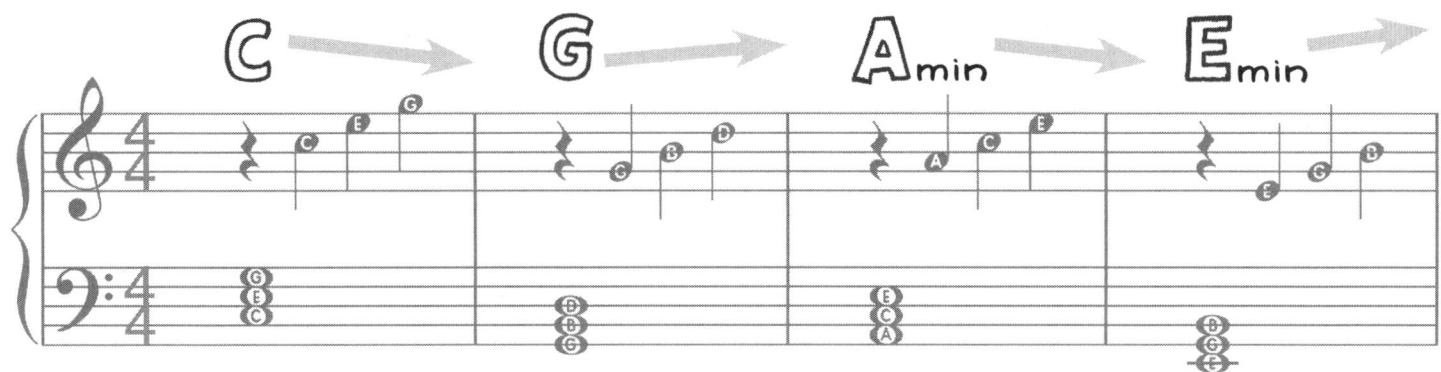

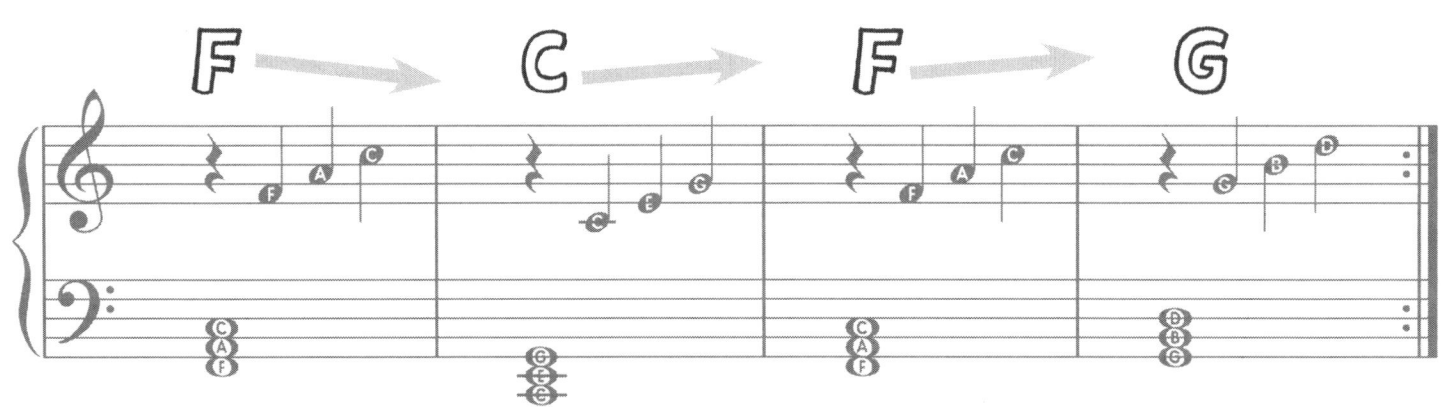

ADD SOME ARTISTRY!

- PLAY LOUDLY AND DRAMATICALLY
- ADD PEDAL
- RH HIGH
- WRITE AN INTRO
- MAKE UP YOUR OWN PATTERN
- PLAY SOFTLY AND EXPRESSIVELY
- LH LOW
- SING "OOHS" AND "AHS"
- CHANGE THE RHYTHM
- CREATE A BOLD ENDING
- ADD A SOLO
- PLAY SMOOTHLY - LIKE A DREAM
- TRY DIFFERENT TEMPOS
- WRITE WORDS

ARTISTRY

Chord Concert: Pachelbel

24. PATTERN 5: CHORD, CHORD

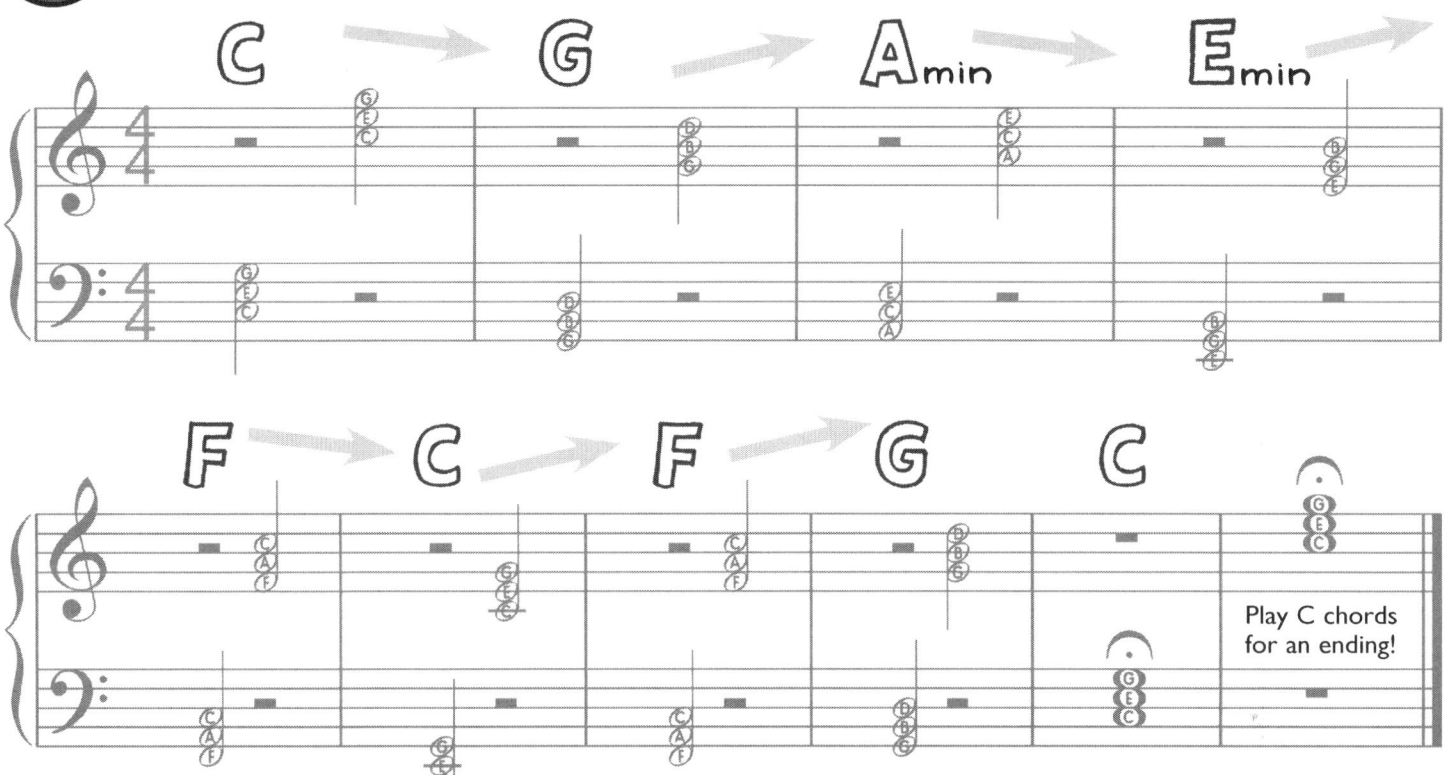

Play C chords for an ending!

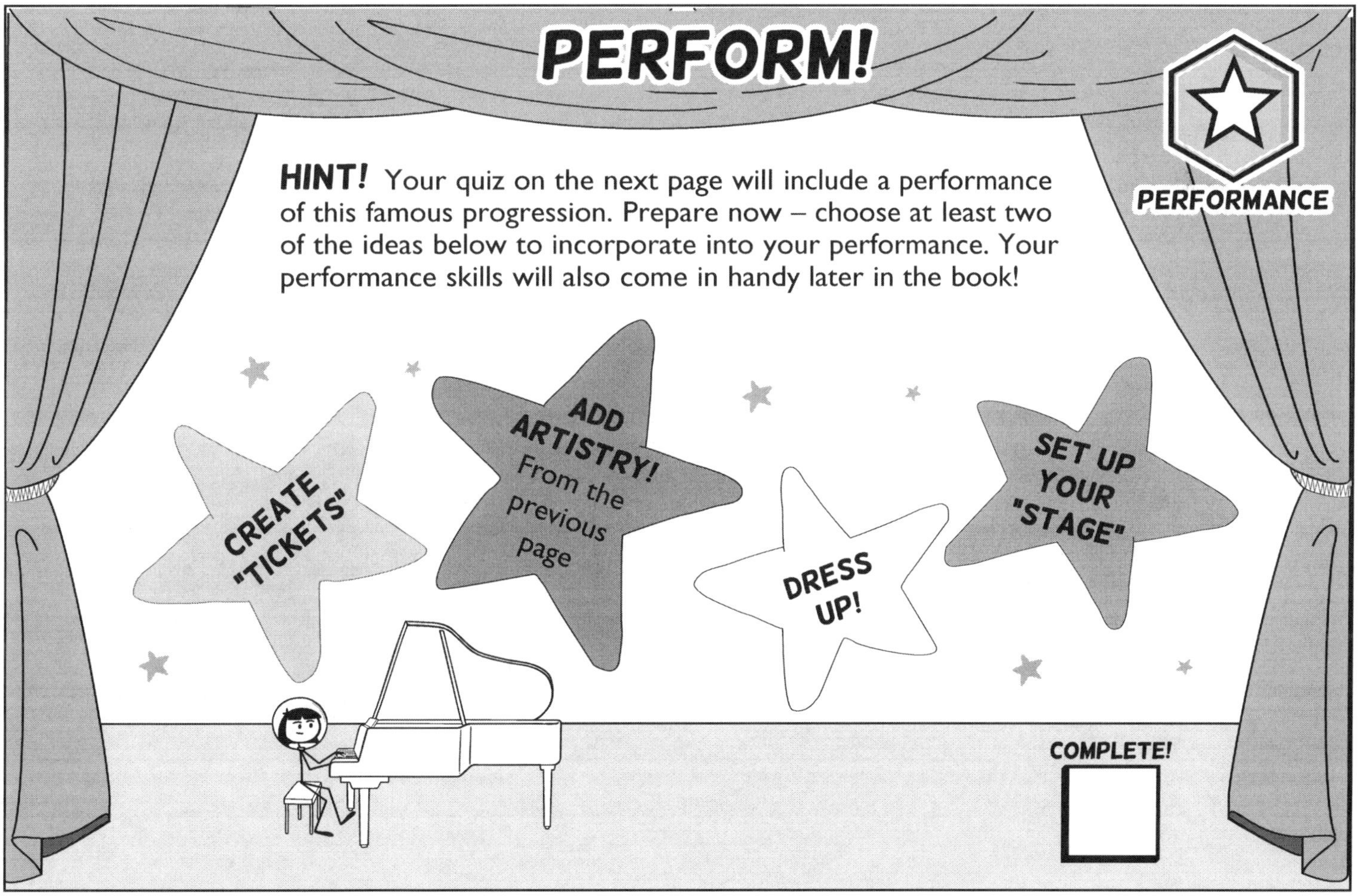

PERFORM!

HINT! Your quiz on the next page will include a performance of this famous progression. Prepare now – choose at least two of the ideas below to incorporate into your performance. Your performance skills will also come in handy later in the book!

PERFORMANCE

- CREATE "TICKETS"
- ADD ARTISTRY! From the previous page
- DRESS UP!
- SET UP YOUR "STAGE"

COMPLETE!

Chord Concert: Pachelbel

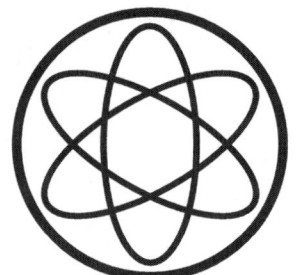

QUANTUM QUIZ!

1 PLAY THE PACHELBEL PROGRESSION FROM MEMORY 3 WAYS

1: _____ COMPLETE! ☐

2: _____ COMPLETE! ☐

3: _____ COMPLETE! ☐

2 NOW GIVE A CONCERT FOR FRIENDS OR FAMILY

Don't forget to add some artistry!

Notes (songs performed, audience comments, etc.)

_____

_____ COMPLETE! ☐

_____

AMAZING PERFORMANCE! And you earned more powers.

We sounded incredible!

It's easy to play, but sounds hard! Let's learn more tricks like that!

COMMAND CENTER

Pattern Powers

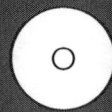 ROOT	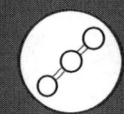 ARPEGGIO
 MALAGUENA POWER PROGRESSION	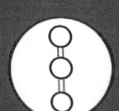 CHORDS
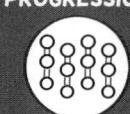 PROGRESSION	 PACHELBEL POWER PROGRESSION
 CROSSOVER ARPEGGIOS 🔒	 INTERVALS 🔒
 FIFTHS 🔒	 MAJOR/MINOR 🔒

Creative Powers

 EXPLORE	 CREATIVITY
 LISTENING	 EXPERIMENT
 ARTISTRY	 PERFORMANCE
 IMPROVISE 🔒	 RHYTHM 🔒
 KNOWLEDGE 🔒	 SONGWRITING 🔒

Chord Concert: Pachelbel

CHAPTER 5
CROSSOVER ARPEGGIOS

"That concert was impressive!"

"You thought that was impressive? Then do I have a trick for you!"

"CROSSOVER ARPEGGIOS!"

"Left, right, left, right Over, under, over, under!"

Get ready to learn an astronmically impressive arpeggio trick. (Psst – don't tell anyone, but it's actually really easy.)

Crossover arpeggios combine your existing arpeggio knowledge with a little fancy hand switching. The result? A great, full sound! Let's give it a try!

WHAT IS A CROSSOVER ARPEGGIO?

PLAY EACH FINGER ONE AT A TIME...

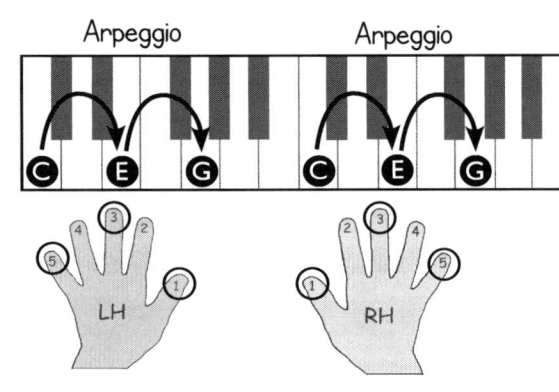

- Place your hands in low C position.
- Play a LH arpeggio and then a RH arpeggio.

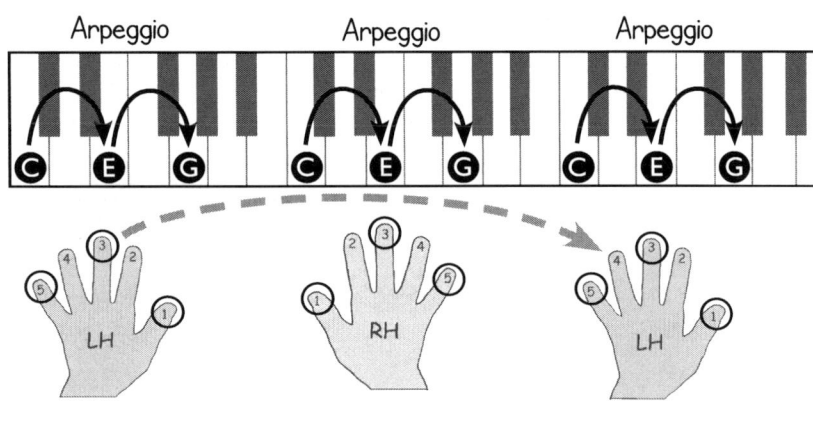

- Cross your LH over your RH, and play another C arpeggio. (Start moving your LH before your RH finishes.)

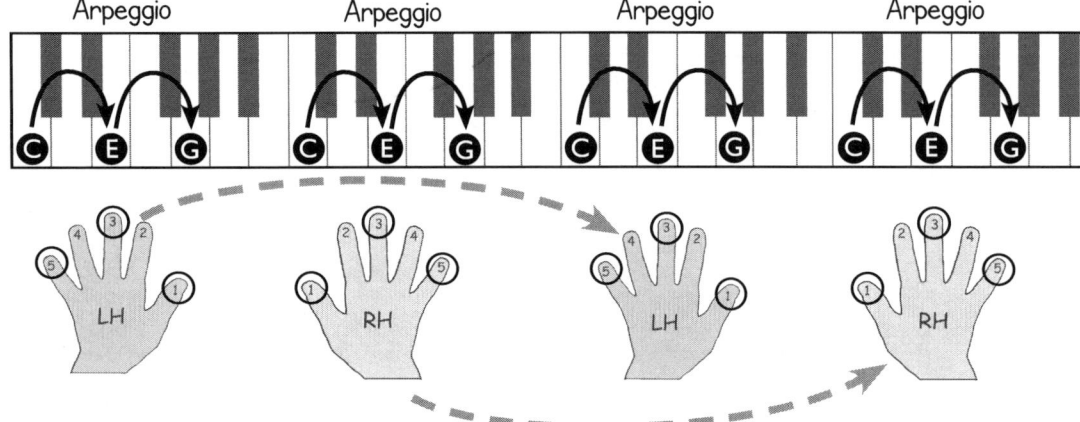

- Finish by crossing your RH under your LH to play the last C arpeggio.

25 CROSSOVER ARPEGGIO SCALE

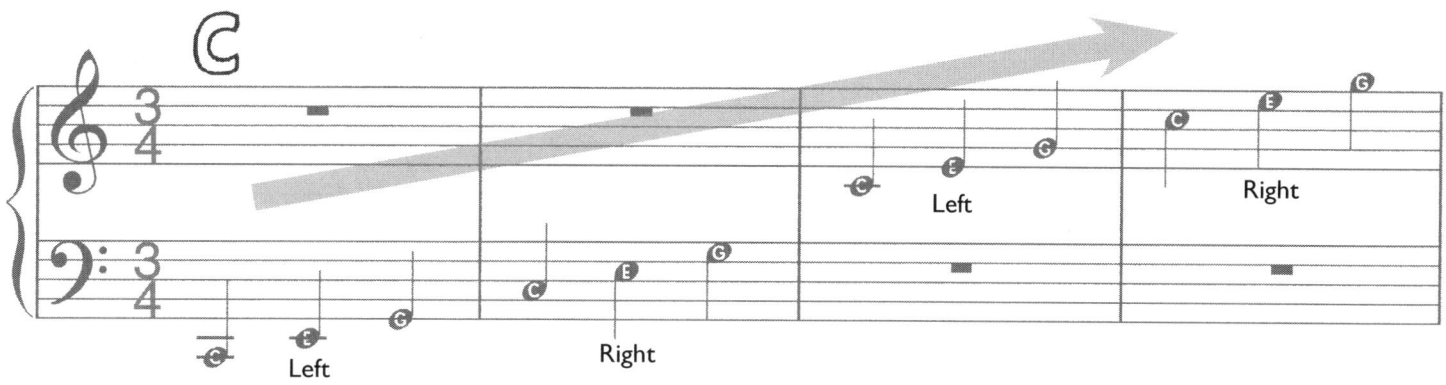

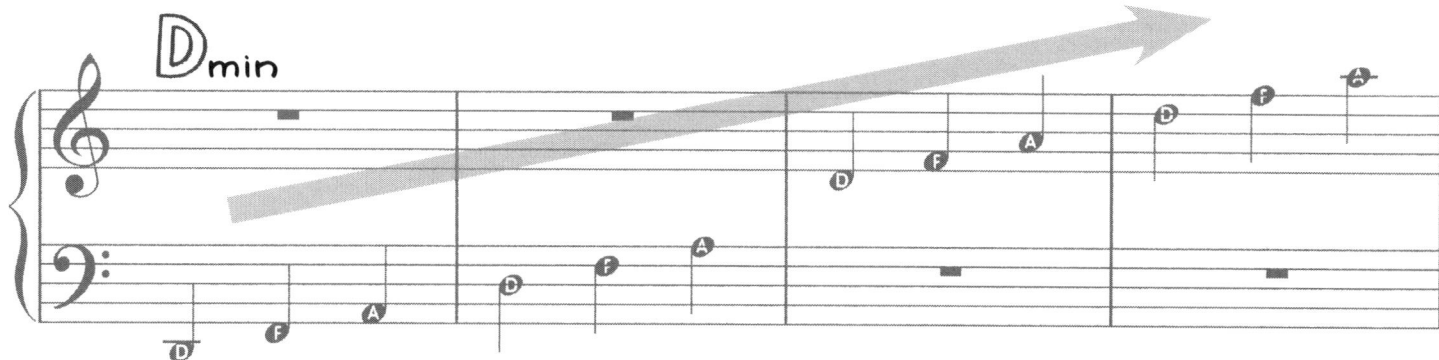

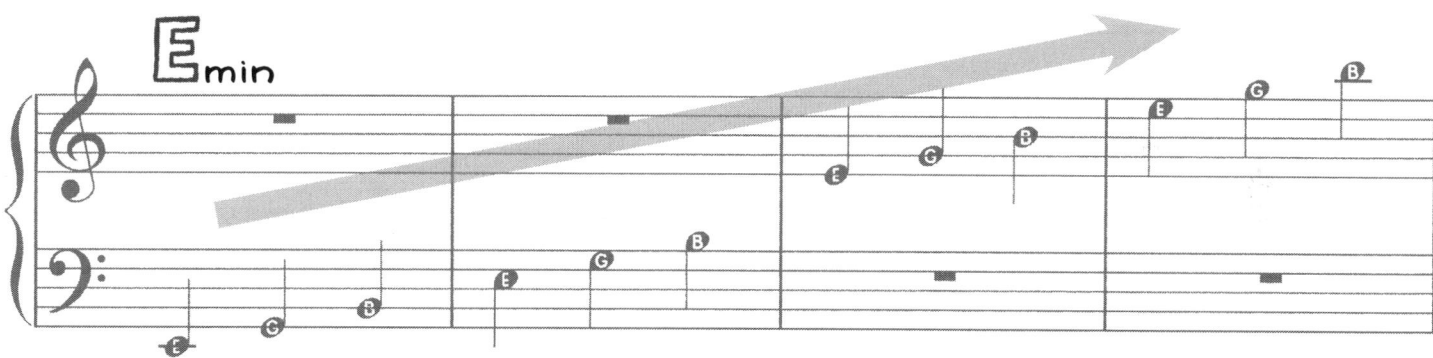

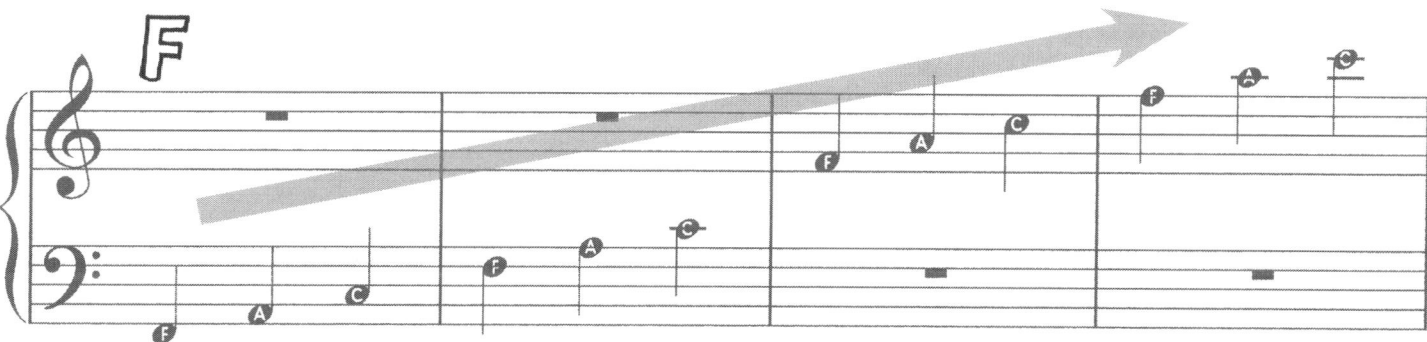

Keep going up the scale. End by playing a high C.

26 MALAGUENA MOONDANCE

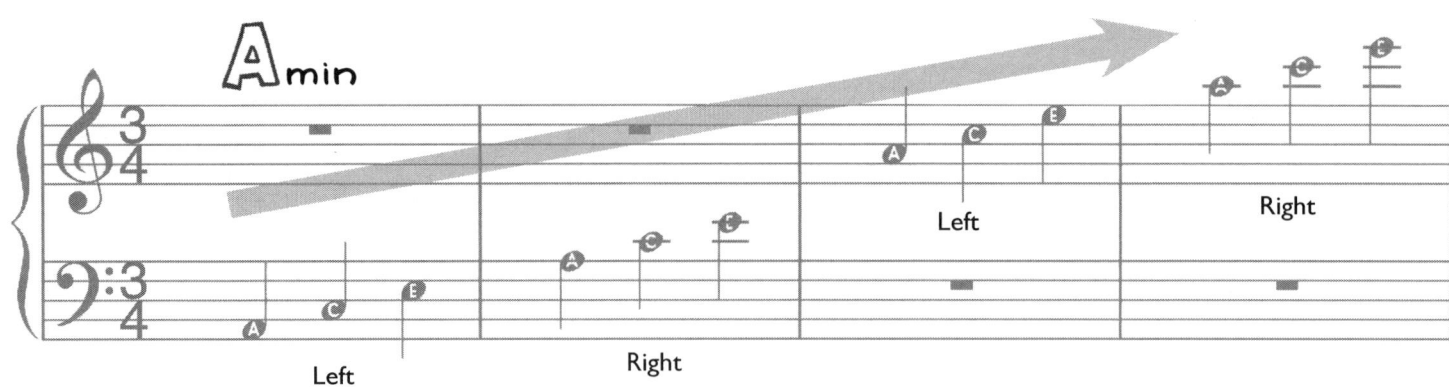

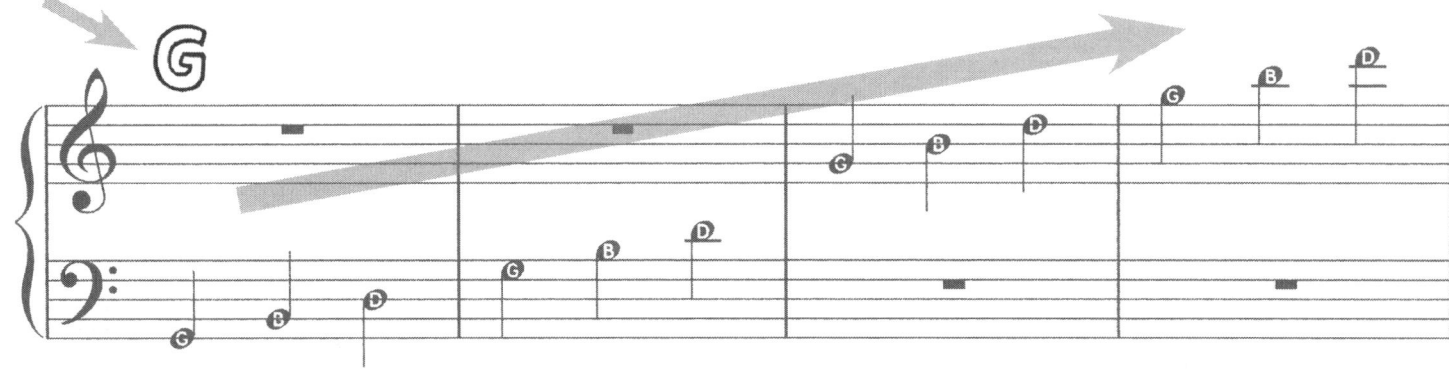

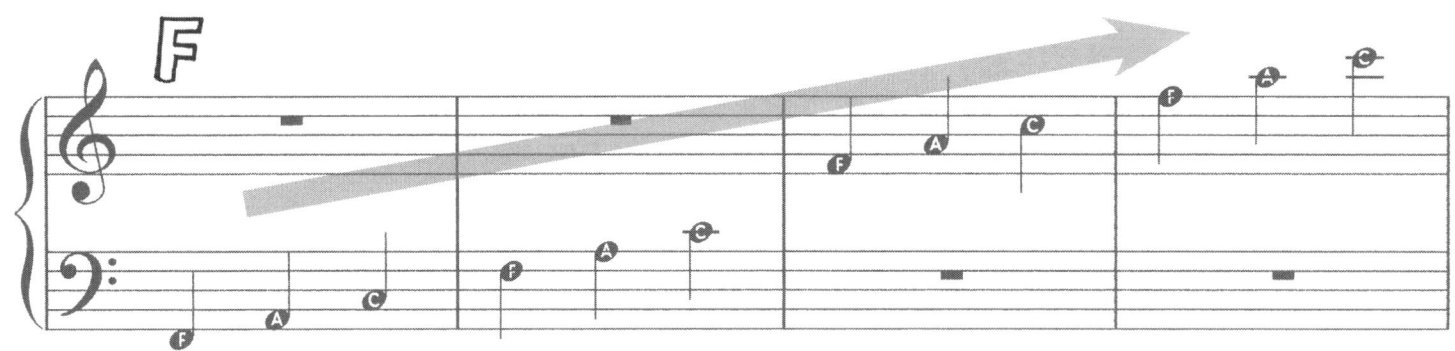

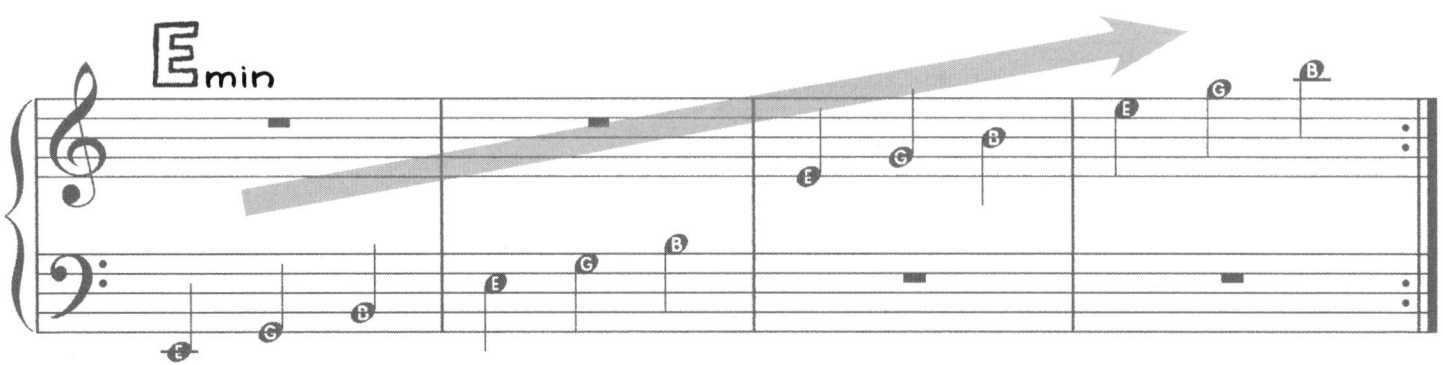

Crossover Arpeggios

27 STARGAZER

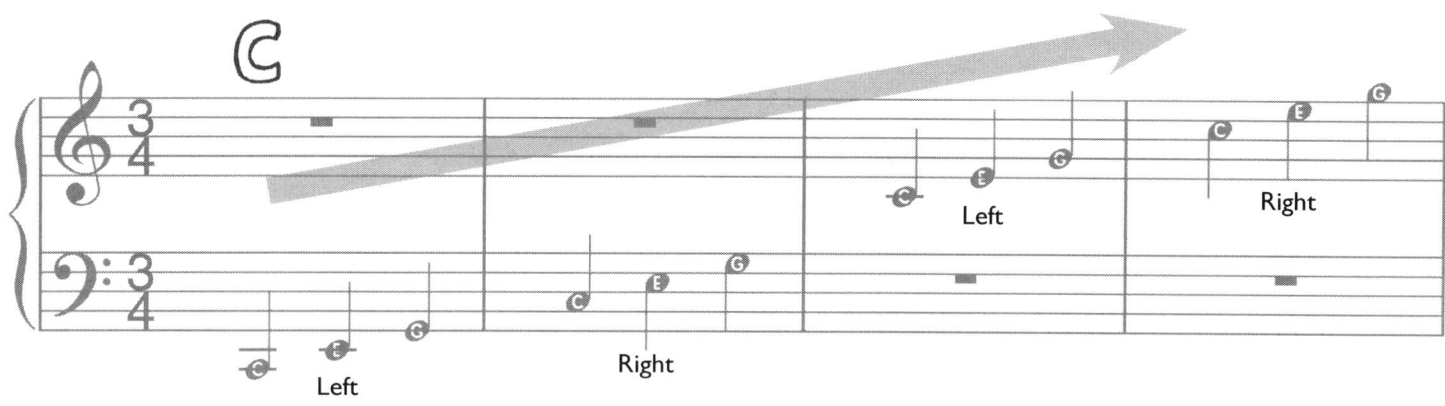
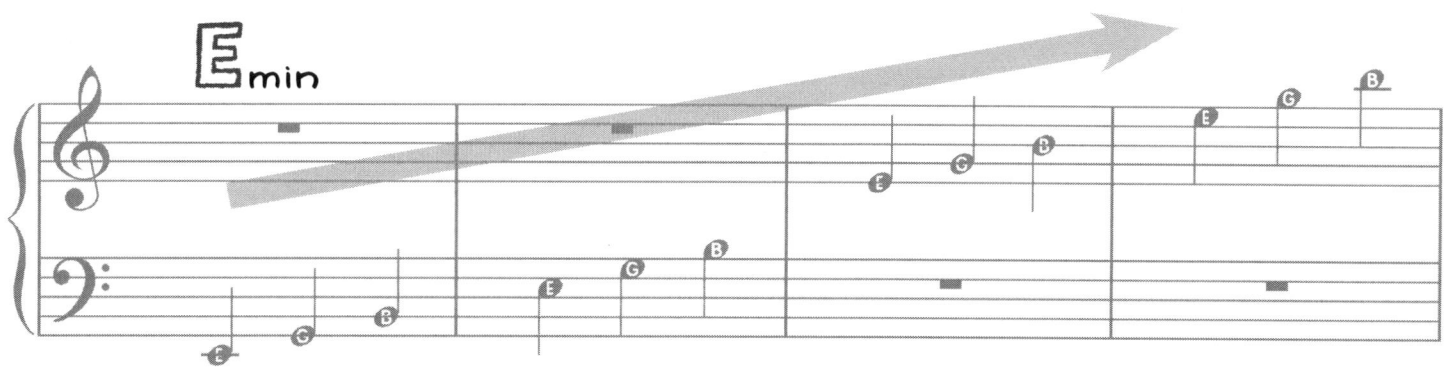
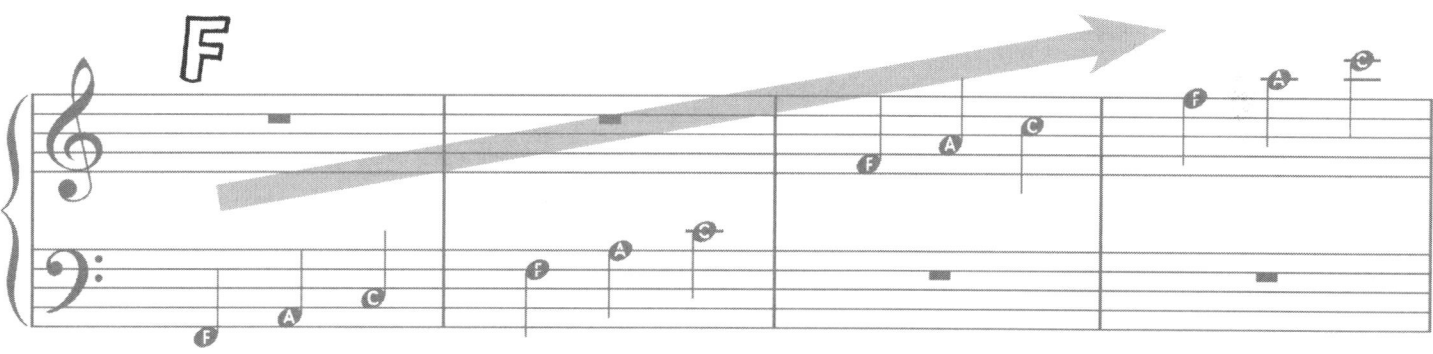
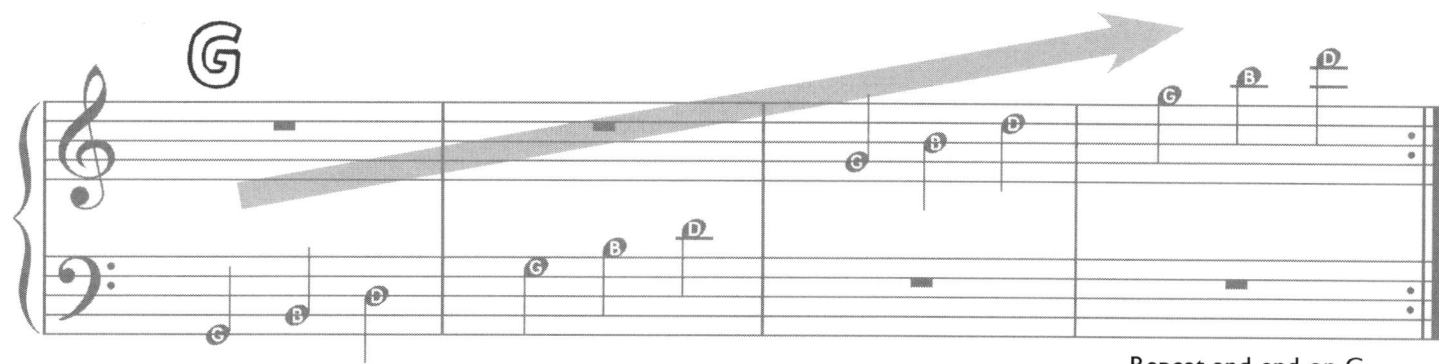

Repeat and end on C

Crossover Arpeggios

28. PACHELBEL POWER-UP

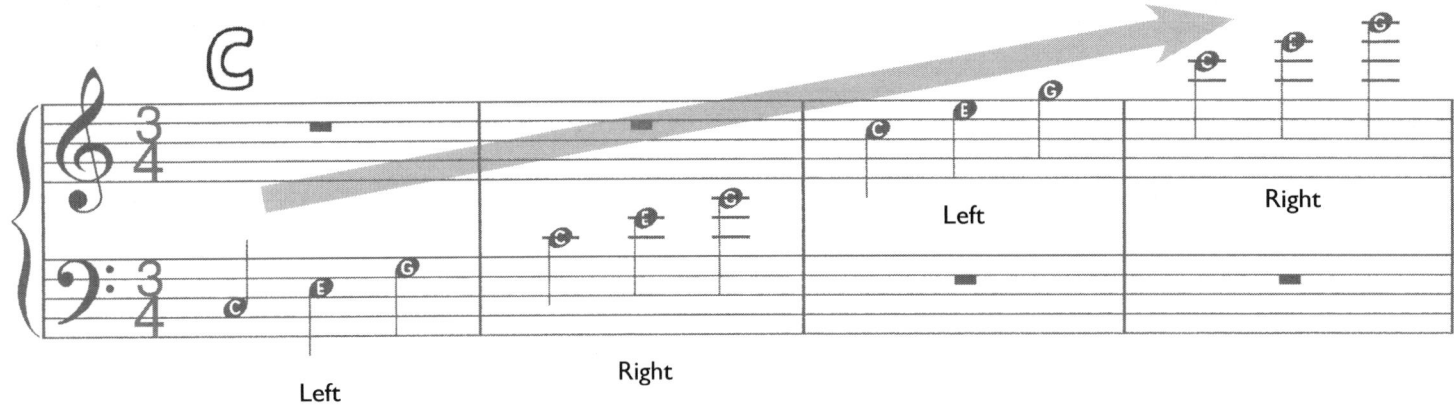
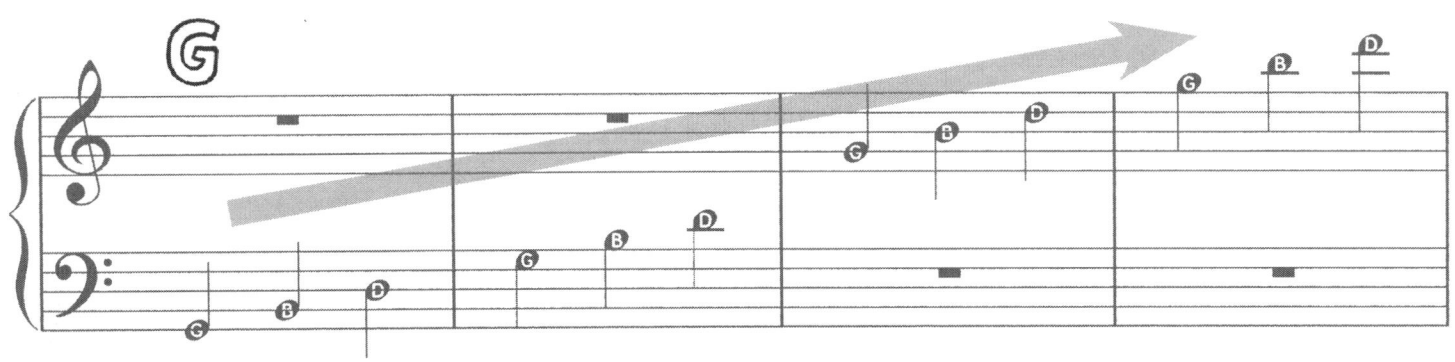
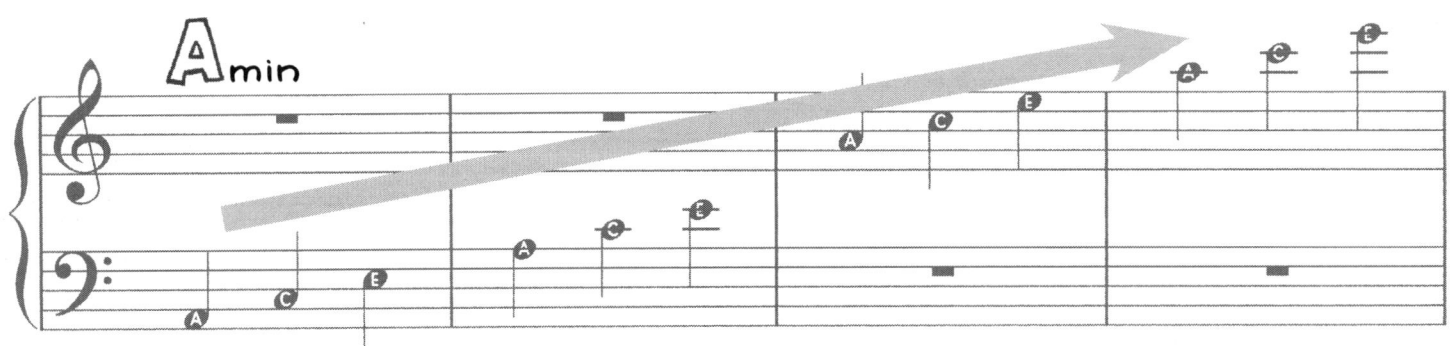
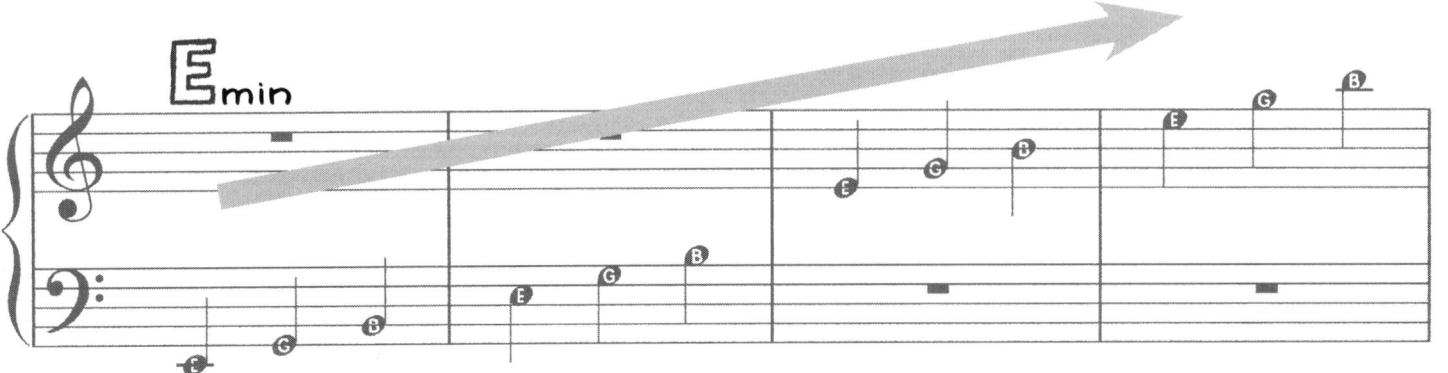

Crossover Arpeggios

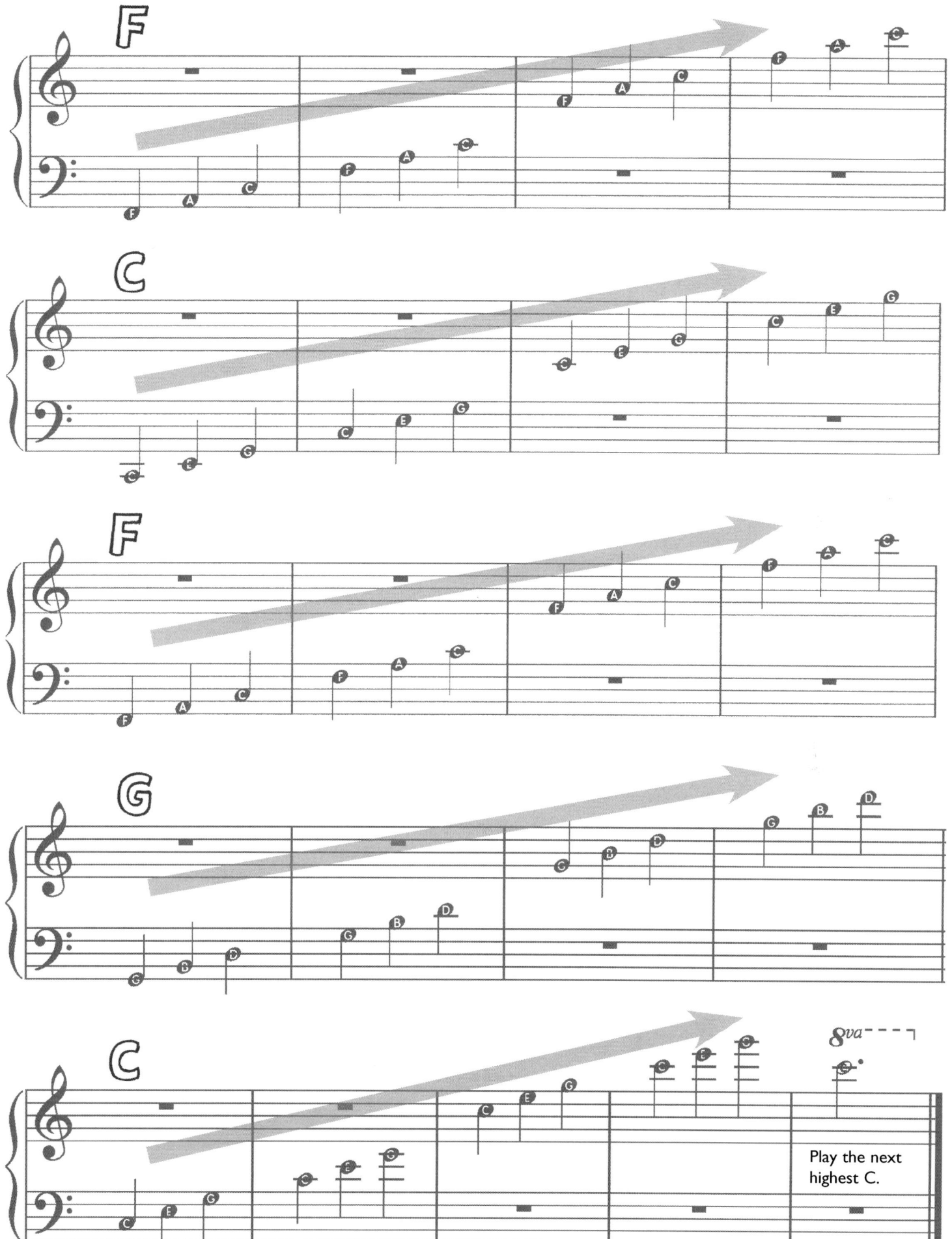

Crossover Arpeggios

57

QUANTUM QUIZ!

1) PLAY! THE CROSSOVER ARPEGGIO SCALE FROM MEMORY   COMPLETE! ☐

2) CREATE!
MAKE YOUR OWN 4 CHORD PROGRESSION HERE. PLAY IT WITH CROSSOVER ARPEGGIOS.

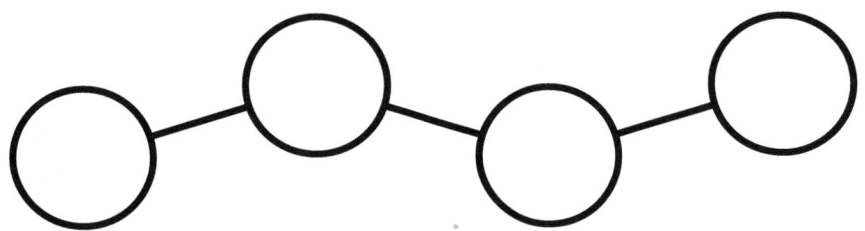

3) PERFORM!

PERFORM YOUR CHORD PROGRESSION FROM CHALLENGE #2 FOR A FRIEND, FAMILY MEMBER OR YOUR TEACHER. TRY ADDING WORDS, AN ENDING OR NEW SECTIONS!   COMPLETE! ☐

Congratulations! You've earned the "Crossover Arpeggio" power.

Impressive!

Crossovers conquered!

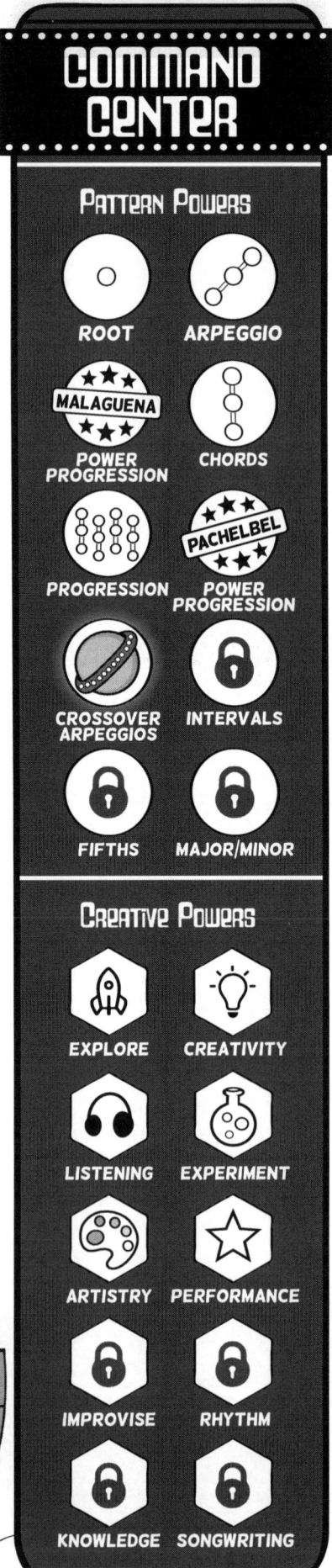

Crossover Arpeggios

CHAPTER 6
INTERVALS

Congratulations! You've traveled so far and learned so much. You are now ready to master a new concept: intervals.

If you completed Meridee's Super Start! My First Piano Patterns book, you will remember some intervals from Planet Plunk - seconds and thirds!

An interval is the relationship (or distance) between two notes or pitches. Think of them as stepping stones that allow us to make music. Each type of interval has its own distinct personality and sound. Get ready to meet them, and see how they work together to make incredible music!

SECONDS

PRACTICE PLAYING SECONDS...

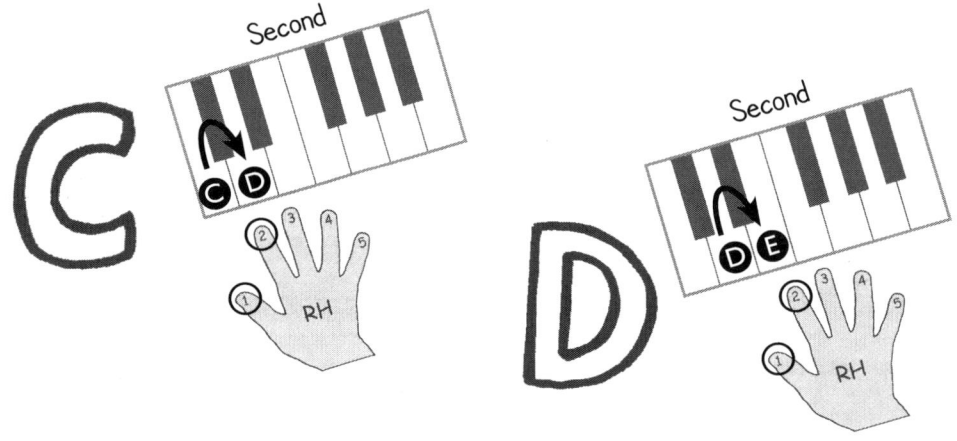

They can be played one at a time (a melodic 2nd) or at the same time (a harmonic 2nd).

Melodic Second   Harmonic Second

EXTRA KNOWLEDGE!

There are actually two different types of seconds: major and minor. (Don't worry – you don't need to know the difference to play these exercises!) A major second is also called a whole step, and a minor second is called a half step. Look it up, or ask your teacher to show you the difference between the two!

29) TOCCATA IN SECONDS

In this exercise, you will be moving up the keyboard playing melodic seconds with your RH, while your LH stays planted on A.

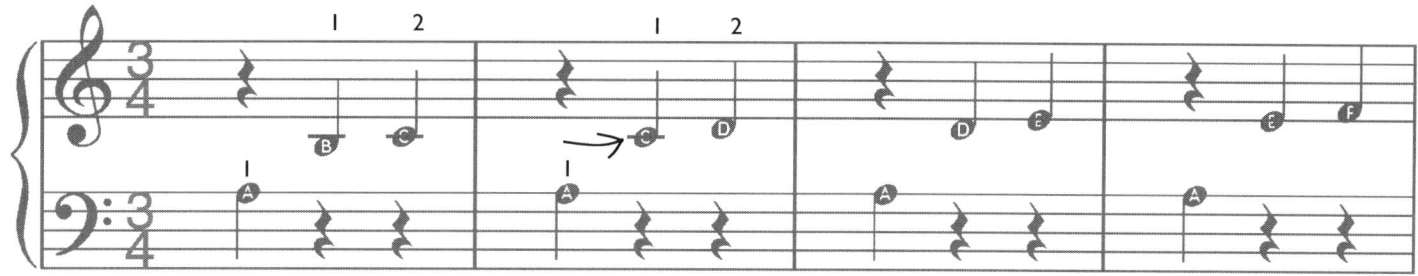

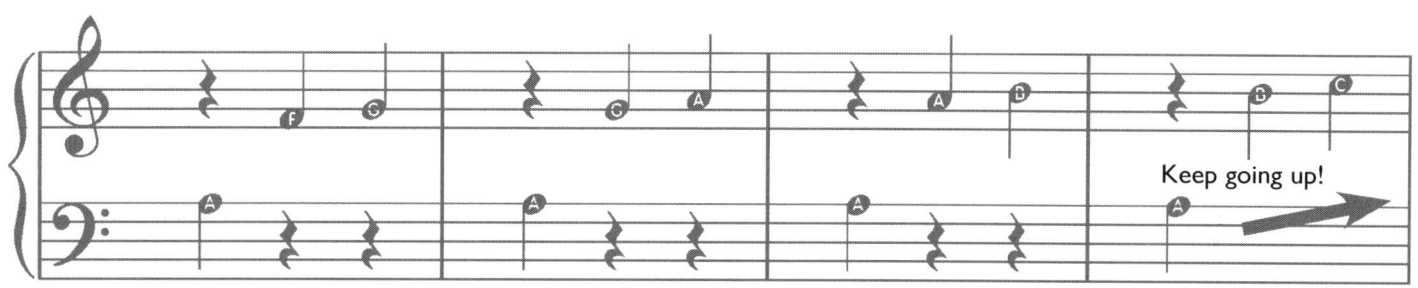

30) WALTZ OF WONDER

In this exercise, your RH will stay put, playing a harmonic second with F and G. Your LH will change every measure - watch out!

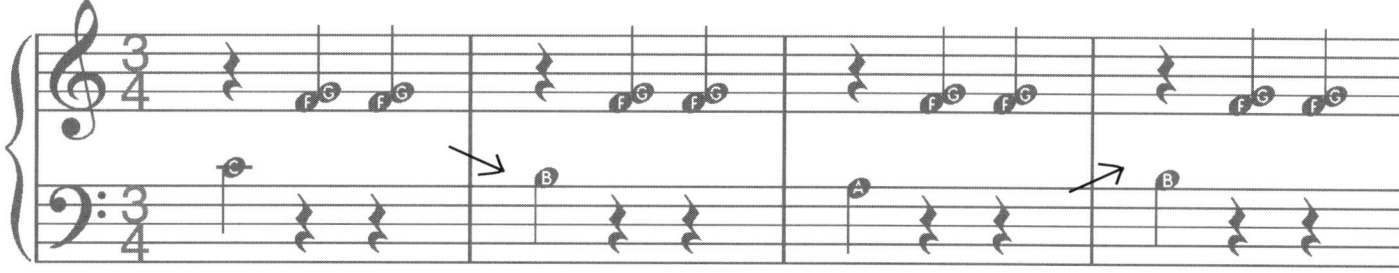

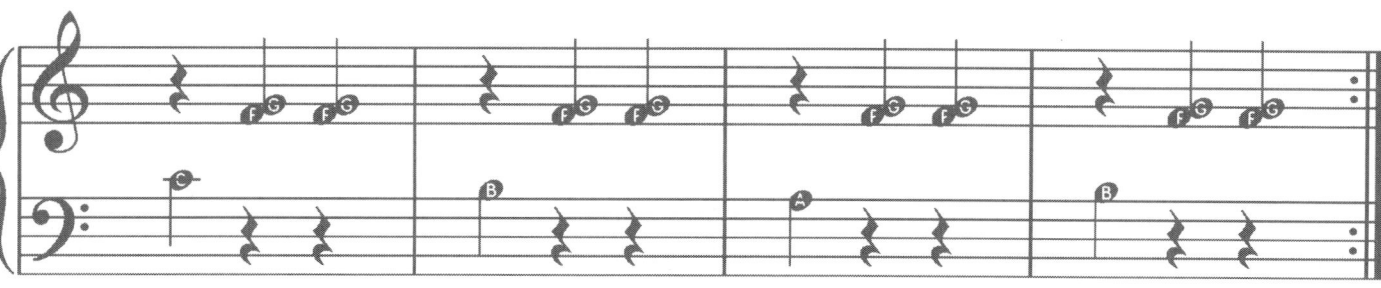

Intervals

MELODIC THIRDS

PRACTICE PLAYING MELODIC THIRDS

First with your left hand...

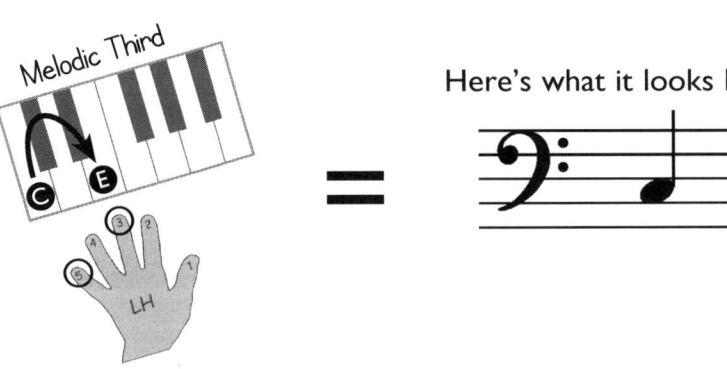

Here's what it looks like on the staff:

Then with your right hand...

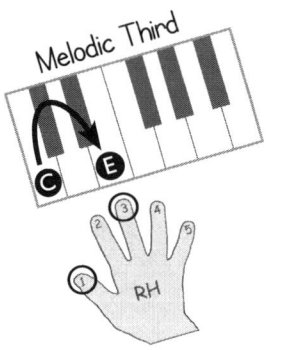

Here's what it looks like on the staff:

EXTRA KNOWLEDGE!

Like seconds, there are two types of thirds: major and minor. You'll get to learn more about them in Chapter 8!

Playing a melodic third is like playing an arpeggio without the top note!

31) PACHELBEL WITH THIRDS

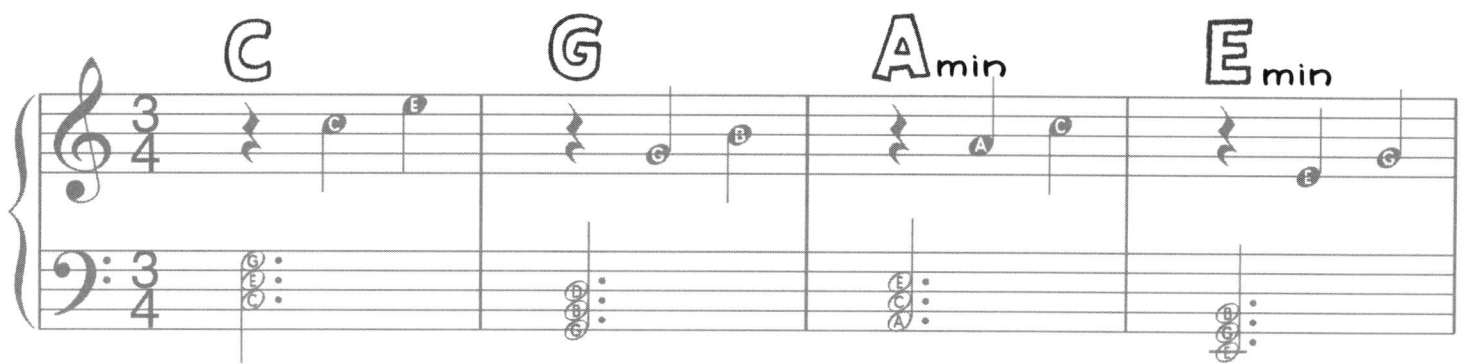
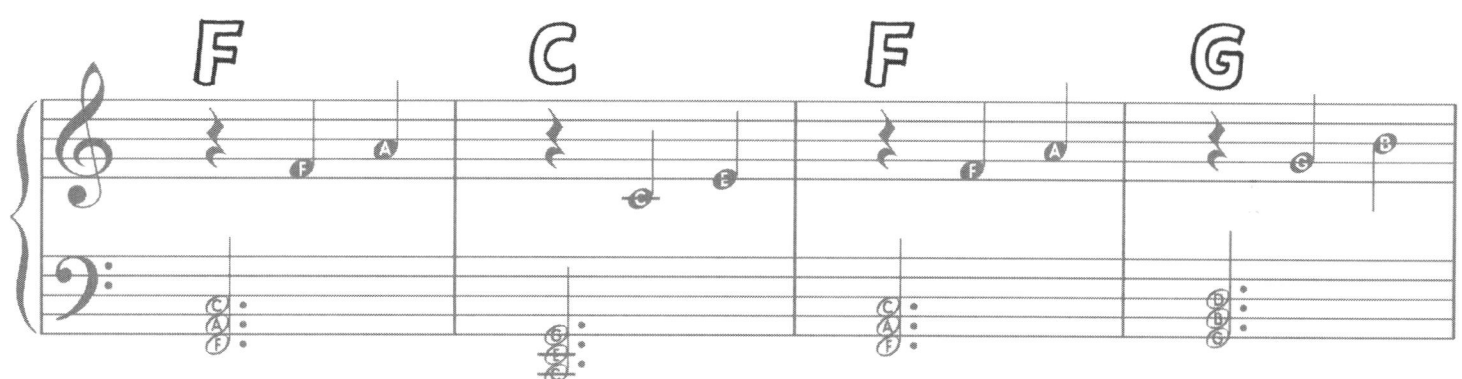
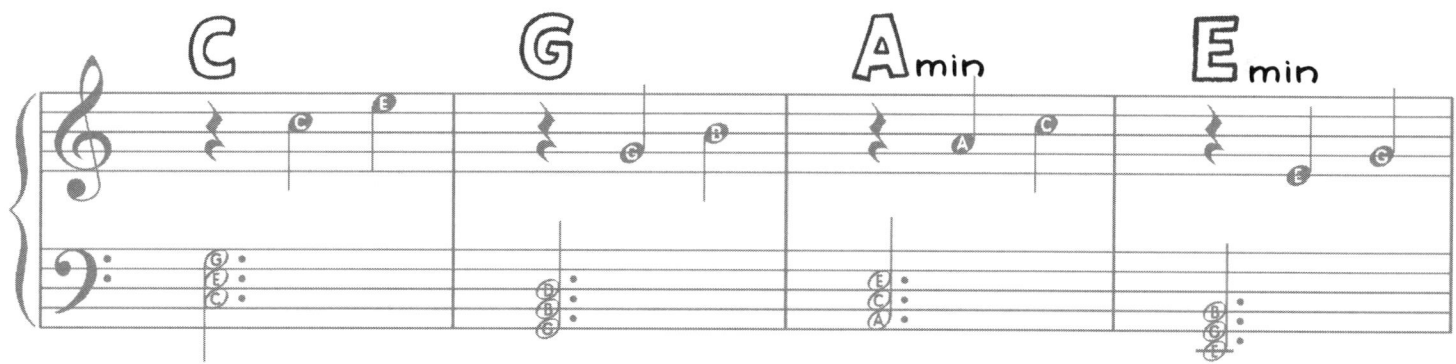
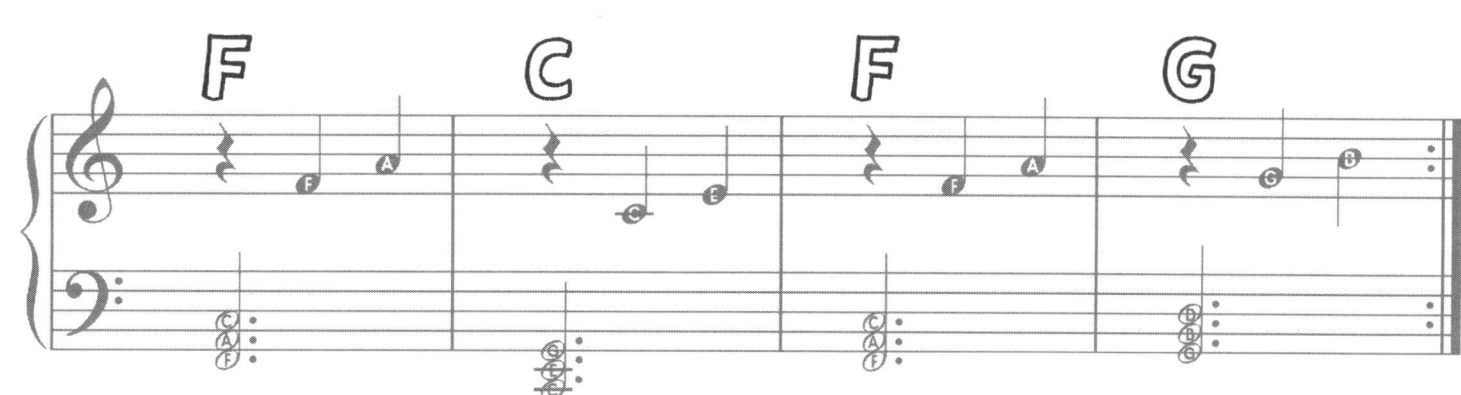

Intervals

HARMONIC THIRDS

PREPARE HANDS...

- Place hands in F position.
- LH plays an arpeggio.
- RH follows by playing a harmonic third (fingers 1 and 3 at the same time).
- Move hands up to G position and repeat.
- Continue the pattern all the way through the progression.

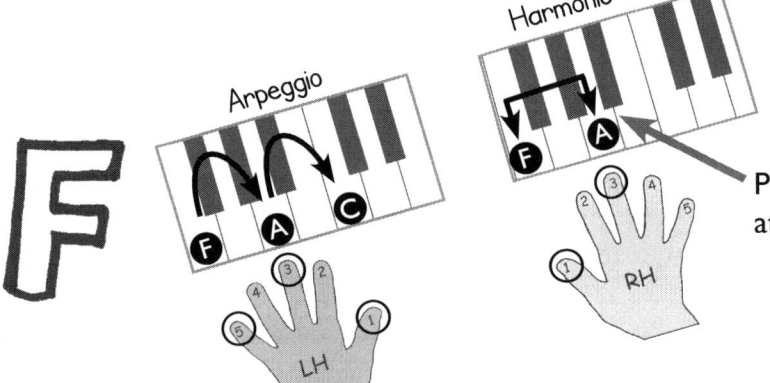

Play both notes at the same time.

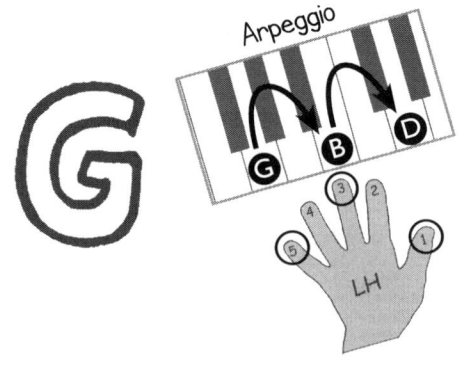

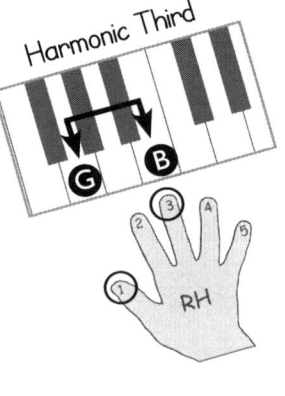

Playing a harmonic third is like playing a chord without the top note.

Intervals

32 DREAMING CLOUDS

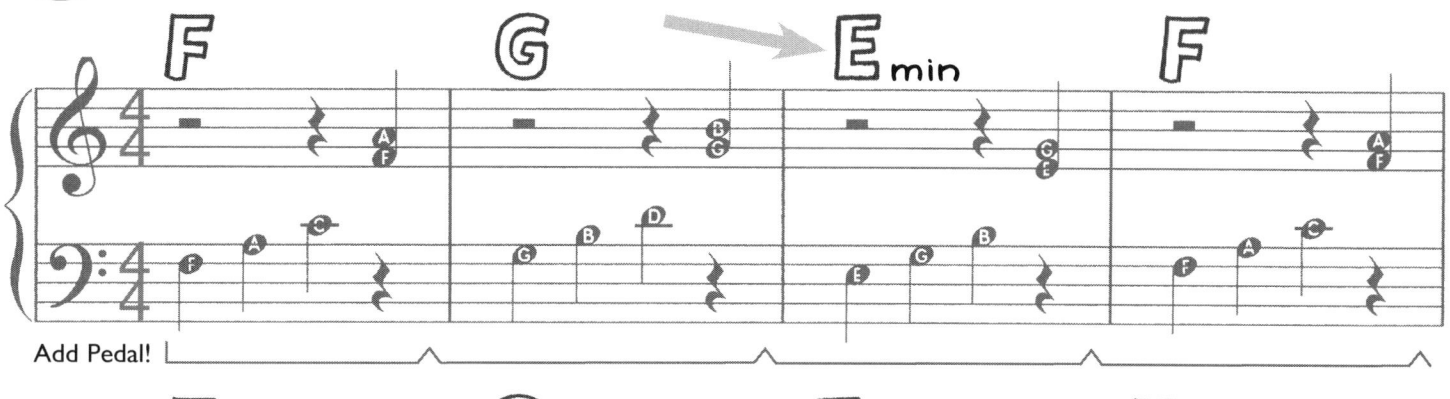

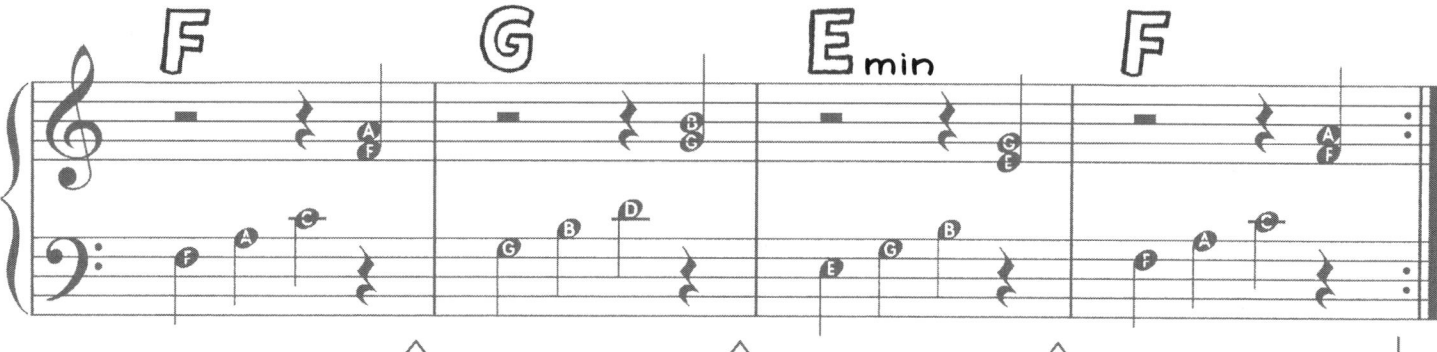

33 DREAMING IMPROV

Play an F arpeggio with your left hand while moving around your right hand to improvise with thirds. Try adding pedal for an extra dreamy effect.

IMPROVISE

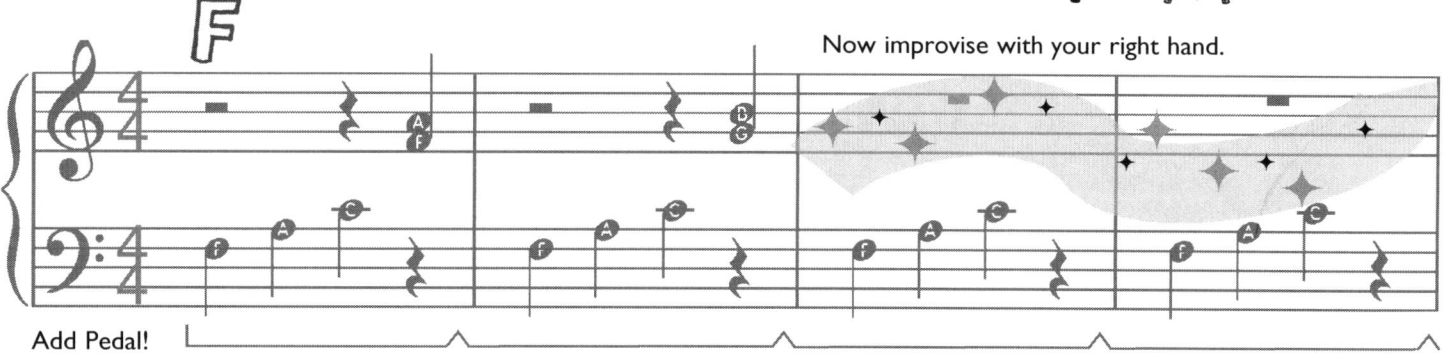

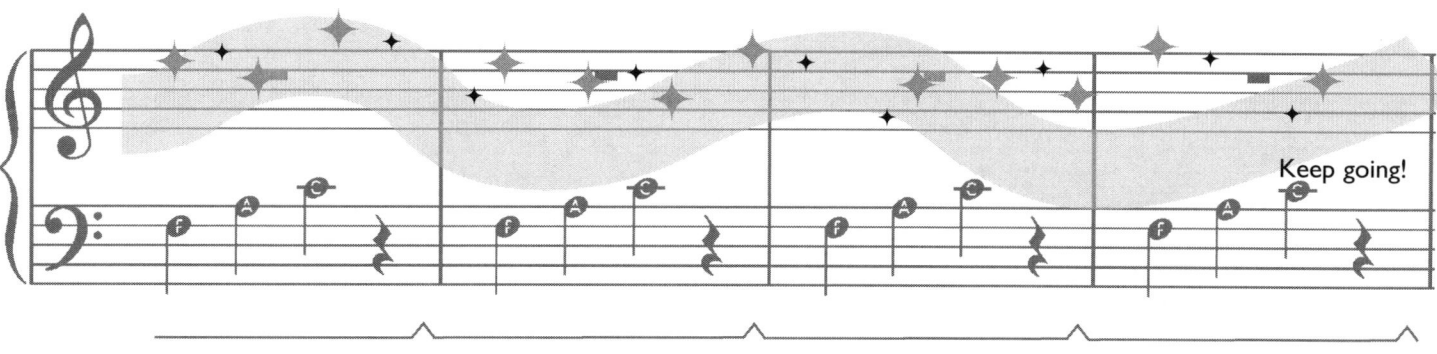

Intervals

FOURTHS

PRACTICE PLAYING A HARMONIC FOURTH...

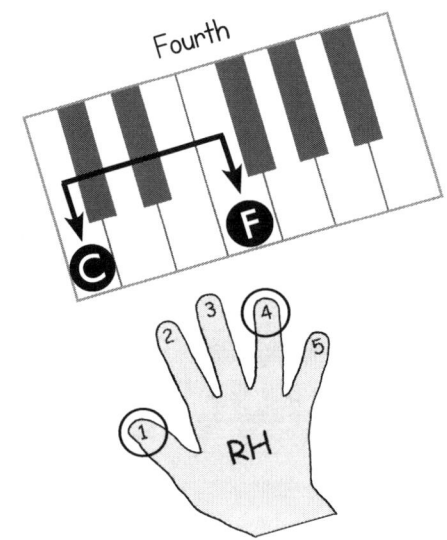

HERE IS WHAT IT LOOKS LIKE ON THE STAFF:

EXTRA KNOWLEDGE!

When we say "fourth" here, we are referring to what is technically known as a "perfect fourth." There is also a less common type of fourth known as the "tritone." The distance between the two notes in the tritone is an additional half step, and it was practically banned from classical music! If you're curious, ask your teacher to play you a tritone. How does it sound compared to a perfect fourth?

34 SPACE CHOPPER

Listen to "Chopsticks" for a similar tune, and check out a Meridee Winters Song Book for even more fun songs!

Right hand starts!

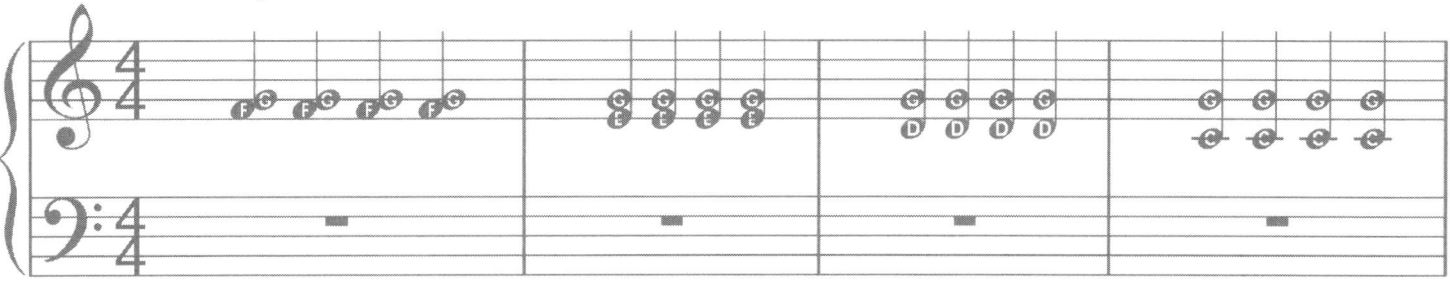

Now the left!

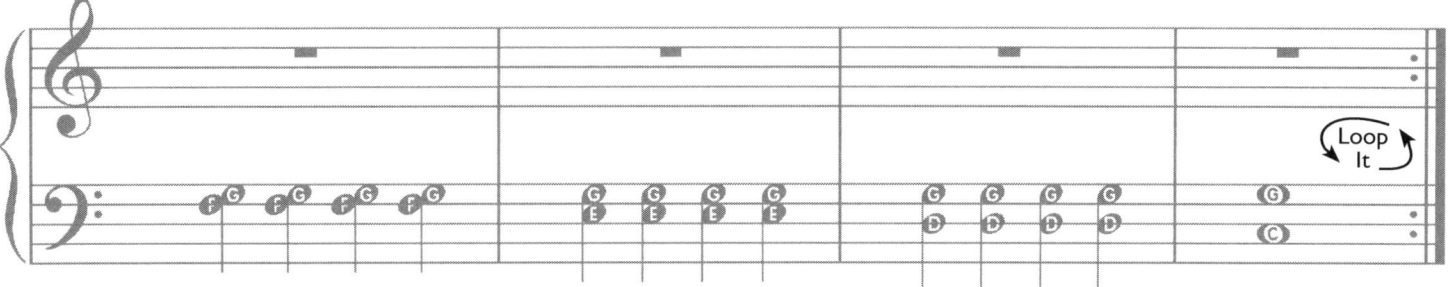

CREATE!

Like we said, each interval has its own personality. Draw a scene here that includes intervals as "characters." (Bonus points if you include that menacing neighbor, a minor second, or that evil villain tritone!)

Intervals

QUANTUM QUIZ!

FOR THIS QUIZ, COMPLETE THIS GAME IN ONE (OR ALL!) OF THE WAYS LISTED:

- The teacher plays an interval, and you name which interval it is. (Bonus challenge: close your eyes and try to name it by listening!)
- Point and play! Close your eyes, point to an interval, and play it!
- Pick a starting note, then build the chosen interval on top of that note.
- Create your own way to play!

COMPLETE! ☐

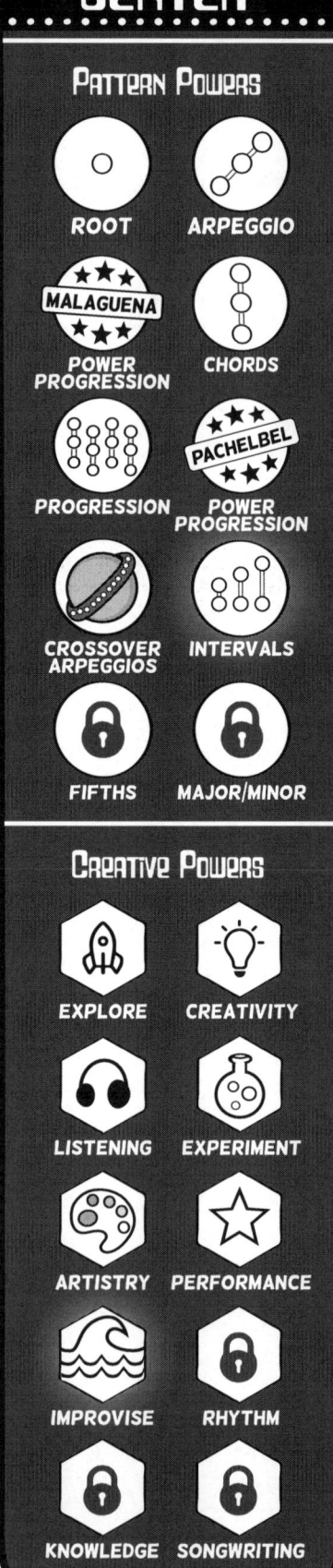

COMMAND CENTER

Pattern Powers
- ROOT
- ARPEGGIO
- MALAGUENA POWER PROGRESSION
- CHORDS
- PROGRESSION
- PACHELBEL POWER PROGRESSION
- CROSSOVER ARPEGGIOS
- INTERVALS
- FIFTHS 🔒
- MAJOR/MINOR 🔒

Creative Powers
- EXPLORE
- CREATIVITY
- LISTENING
- EXPERIMENT
- ARTISTRY
- PERFORMANCE
- IMPROVISE
- RHYTHM 🔒
- KNOWLEDGE 🔒
- SONGWRITING 🔒

"Congratulations! You've earned your Interval and Improvising powers!"

"Sonic Seconds! Thrilling Thirds! Fierce Fourths!"

"Time to fire away with FIFTHS!"

Intervals

CHAPTER 7

POWER CHORDS: FIFTHS

Now it's time to feel the power – the power of fifths! Think of fifths as the heavyweights of music. Why is a fifth a heavyweight interval? Distance. The distance between the notes creates a big, strong sound. This powerful sound creates stability, which is something our ears like. Like fourths and octaves*, the interval of a fifth is known as a "perfect" interval. But don't be deceived – perfect fifths are perfect for rock music!

In this chapter you will learn about fifths, and then use them to create power and strength in your own playing.

Let's get POWERFUL!

PERFECT FIFTHS = MY OTHER FAVORITE INTERVAL

*You're going to majorly rock out with octaves in Chord Quest Level 4. Seriously.

Power Chords: Fifths

MELODIC FIFTHS

MELODIC FIFTHS ARE ARPEGGIOS WITHOUT THE THIRD...

 **LH MELODIC FIFTH**
- Place hands in C position.
- Play C with LH finger 5 (pinky).
- Play G with LH finger 1 (thumb).
- That's a melodic 5th!

 **RH MELODIC FIFTH**
- Play C with your RH finger 1 (thumb).
- Play G with your RH finger 5 (pinky).

 **PRACTICE UNTIL SMOOTH**

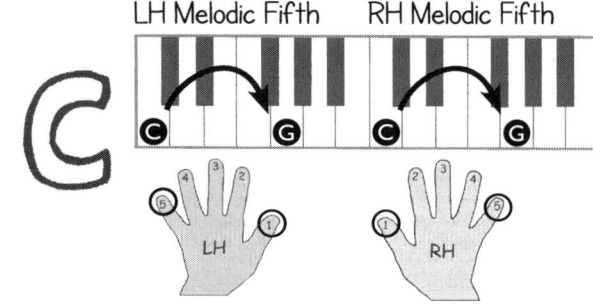

35 DRAGON WARRIOR

Play the melodic fifths pattern starting on D. Say/think: "Left, left, right, right."

Power Chords: Fifths

HARMONIC FIFTHS

Harmonic fifths, a.k.a. "power chords," are the classic heavy metal sound. This pattern has a driving pulse of quarter notes, which is also common in rock and heavy metal.

HARMONIC FIFTHS ARE PLAYED AT THE SAME TIME
(LIKE CHORDS)

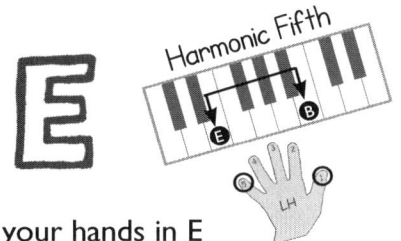

Place your hands in E position. With your LH, play fingers 5 and 1 at the same time. This is a harmonic fifth.

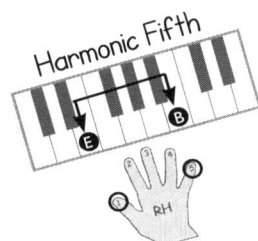

With your RH, echo by playing a harmonic fifth.

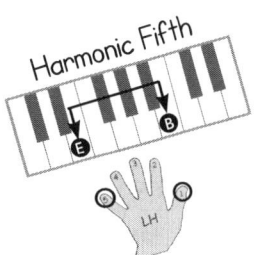

Play your LH again.

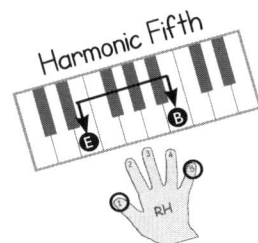

Play your RH again.

36 LUNAR LIGHTNING

"Rock" back and forth between hands.

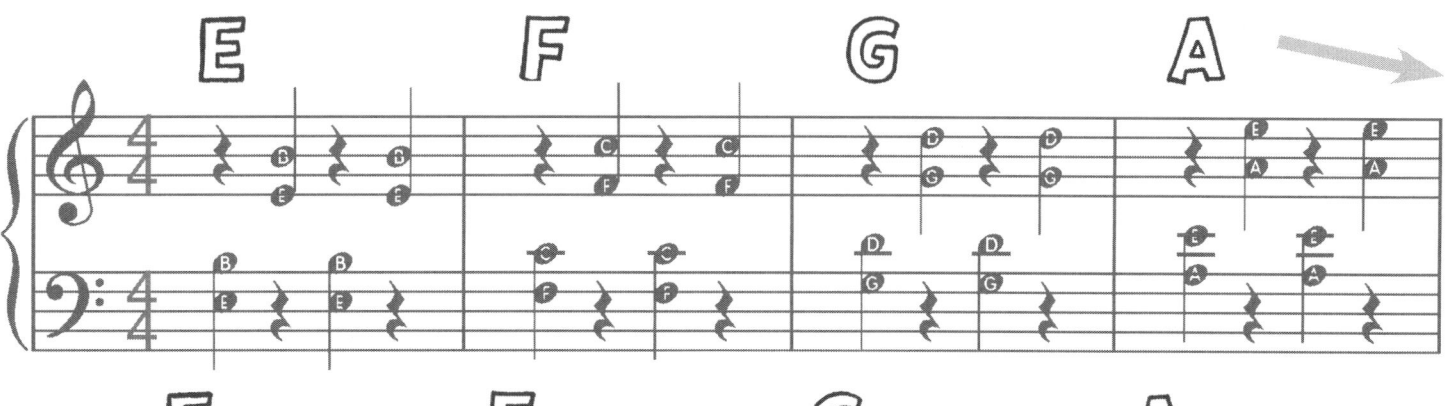

Create a dramatic rock star ending on E!

Power Chords: Fifths

37 MYSTERIOUS MOON

Repeat the ending and fade out.

38 WARRIOR HEART

This song mixes melodic fifths and melodic thirds.

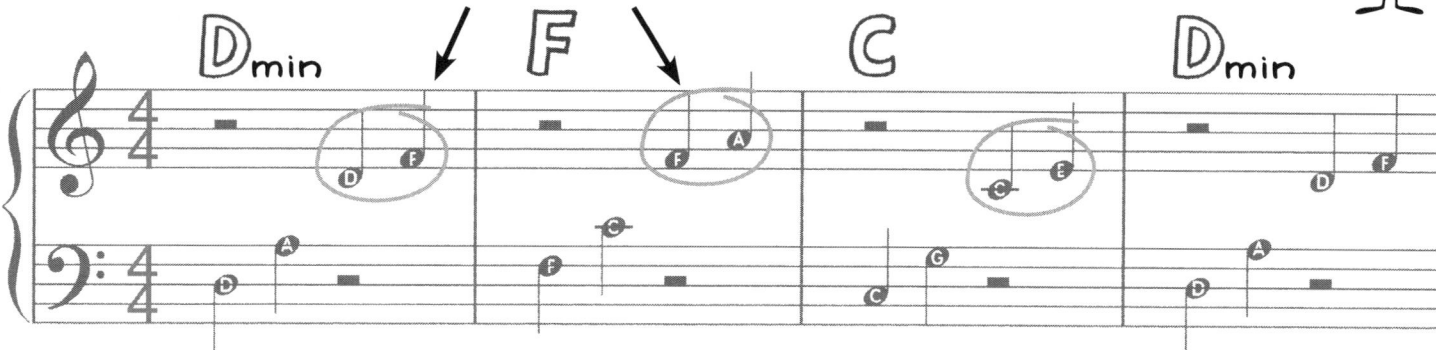

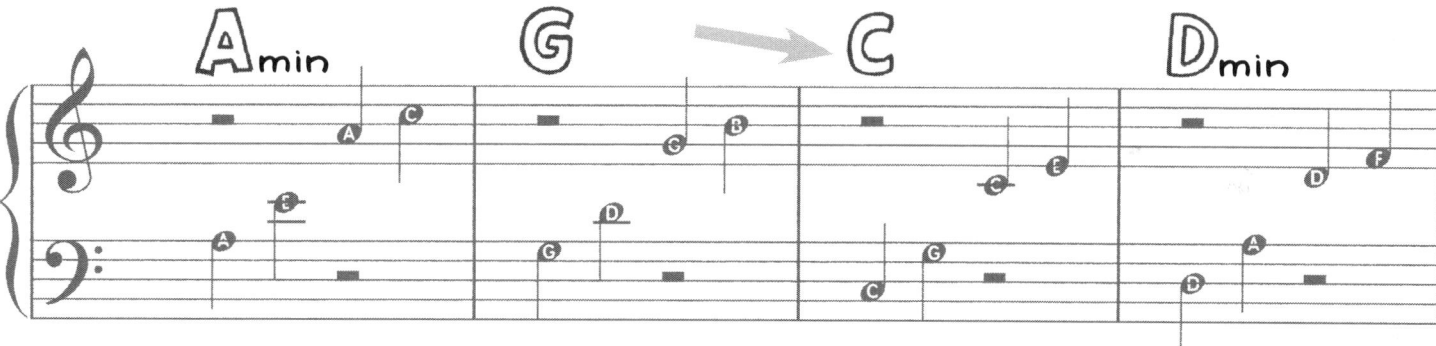

DATE				RHYTHM CHALLENGE
FASTEST				
SLOWEST				

RHYTHM CHALLENGE! Try this exercise with a metronome. Record your best (accurate!) slow and fast tempos here. Try to beat your fastest and slowest tempos!

Power Chords: Fifths

HEART OF ROCK

 Now we are going to take a powerful rock progression and play it 3 different ways.

 What songs use this progression? "Let It Be," "Glycerine," "With or Without You," "No Woman No Cry," "Can You Feel the Love Tonight," and tons more!

 Cool!

PATTERN 1

With your hands in C position, play a melodic fifth with your LH.

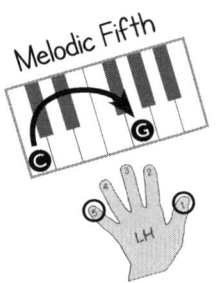

Follow it with a melodic fifth in your RH.

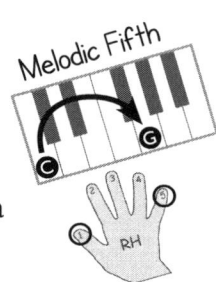

Play this pattern with Heart of Rock 1.

PATTERN 2

Play a melodic fifth with your LH.

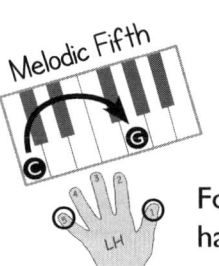

Follow it with a harmonic fifth in your RH. Hold for TWO beats.

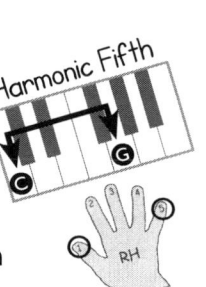

Play this pattern with Heart of Rock 2.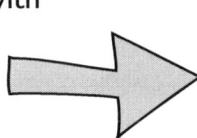

PATTERN 3

Play a harmonic fifth with your LH.

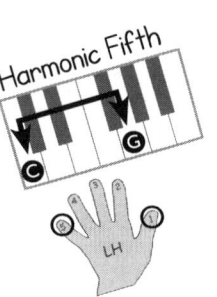

Repeat the LH harmonic fifth.

Follow it with a harmonic fifth in your RH. Hold for TWO beats.

Play this pattern with Heart of Rock 3.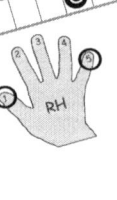

Power Chords: Fifths

39) HEART OF ROCK 1
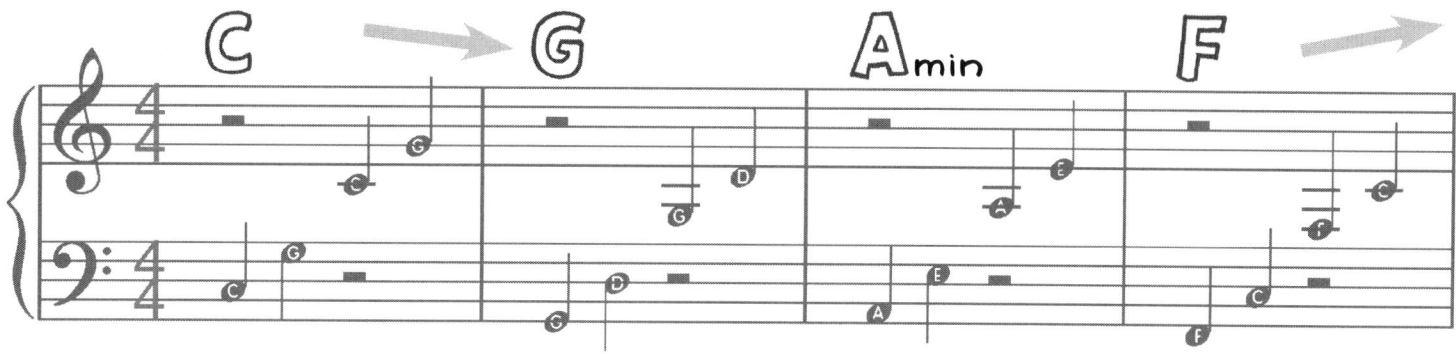

40) HEART OF ROCK 2

41) HEART OF ROCK 3
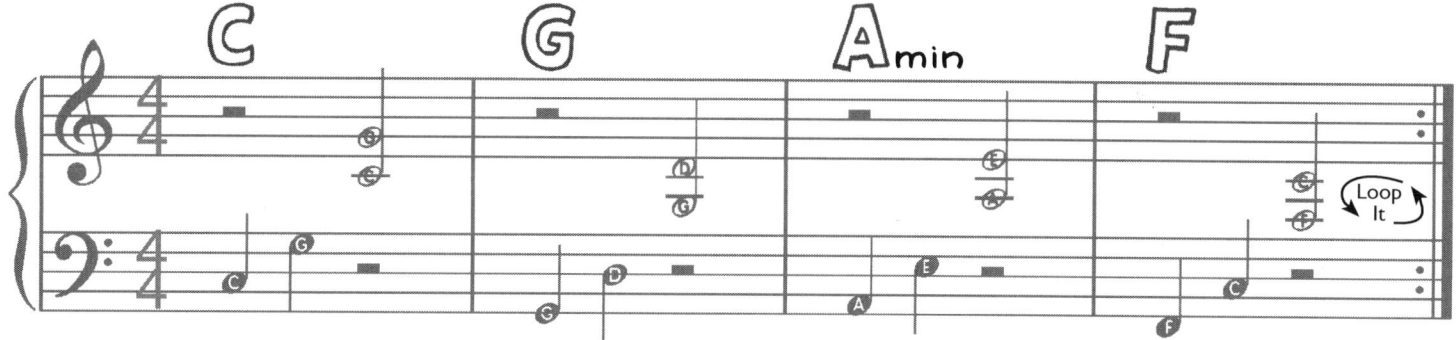

Power Chords: Fifths

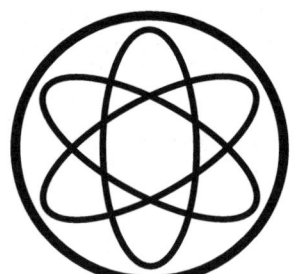  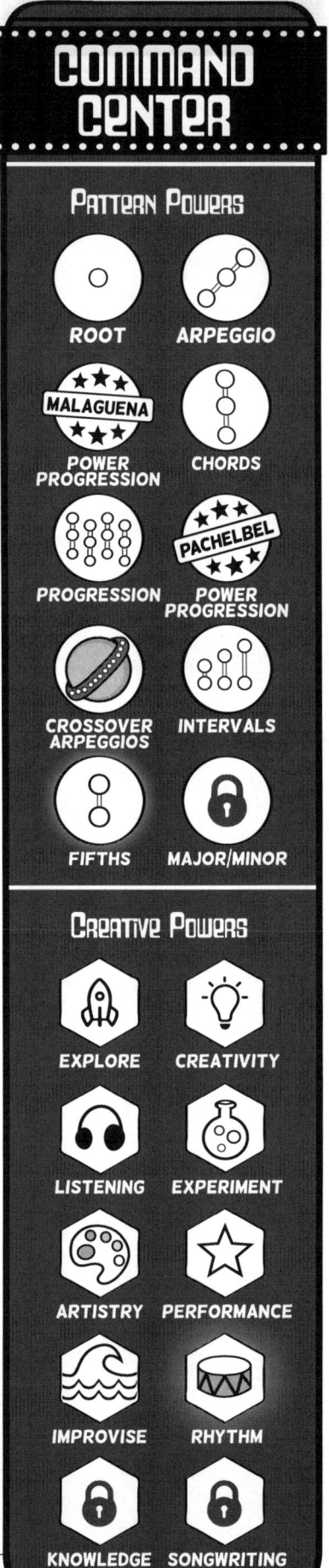

QUANTUM QUIZ!

For this quiz, we're headed back to the lab! Using the choices below, come up with your own chord progressions. Then play them with melodic and harmonic fifths!

1 CHOOSE FROM THESE ROOT NOTES:

Ⓐ Ⓔ Ⓒ Ⓕ Ⓓ Ⓖ

2 WRITE A FEW CHORD PROGRESSIONS OF YOUR OWN

Create your own progression by writing a chord name in each circle. Then try playing them with melodic and harmonic fifths. Lastly, choose one to play to a metronome.

PROGRESSION 1: PLAY WITH MELODIC FIFTHS

○—○—○—○

PROGRESSION 2: PLAY WITH HARMONIC FIFTHS

○—○—○—○

Congratulations! You've earned the powers of fifths and rhythm!

Powerful!

MAJORLY excited for what's next!

Power Chords: Fifths

CHAPTER 8
MAJOR AND MINOR CHORDS

In this chapter you will learn about major and minor chords. While major chords have 4 half-steps between the root and third, minor chords only have 3. You'll learn that changing this one note can make a happy song sad, a cheery song spooky, or vice versa. So, check it out for yourself, and learn the difference that a half-step makes!

Major and Minor Chords

WHAT IS A MAJOR CHORD?

 **MAJOR CHORDS** have 4 half steps between the root and the third.

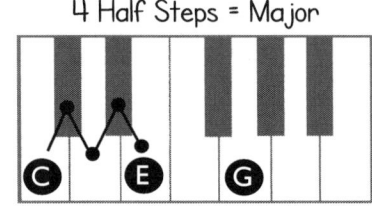

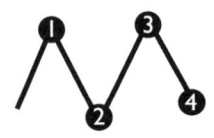

THE MAJOR CHORDS IN THE KEY OF C ARE...

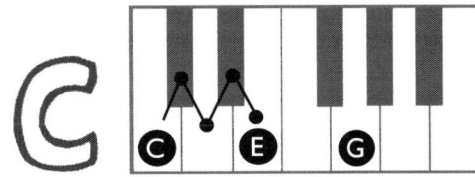

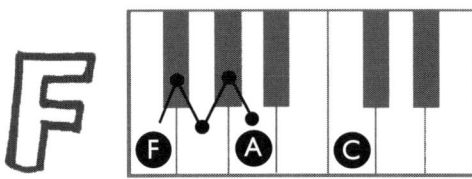

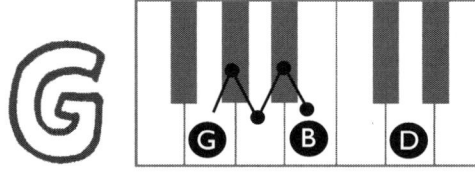

 To learn more about this, check out a music theory book!

Major chords sound happy! Play them and listen.

Major and Minor Chords

WHAT IS A MINOR CHORD?

 **MINOR CHORDS** have 3 half steps between the root and the third.

3 half steps = minor

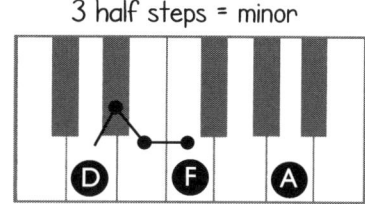 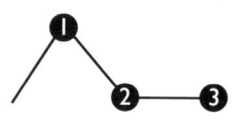

THE MINOR CHORDS IN THE KEY OF C ARE...

 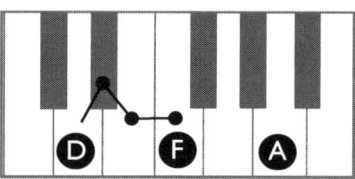

 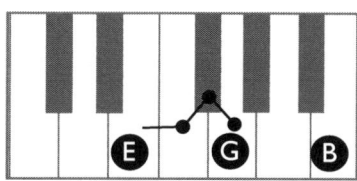

 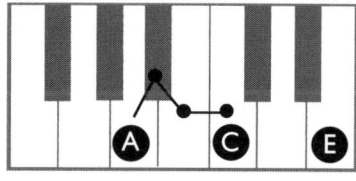

Major and Minor Chords

 MINOR CHORD MASH UP

Minor chords are used in sad songs or mysterious movies. Can you hear why?

 MAJOR CHORD MERRIMENT

Listen to this progression of all major chords. Can you hear the difference from minor? Can you feel the difference?

Major and Minor Chords

MAJOR TO MINOR (BRING IT DOWN...)

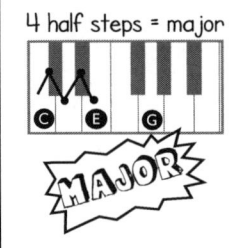
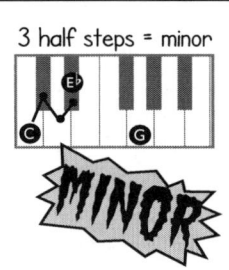

LET'S CHANGE C MAJOR INTO C MINOR...

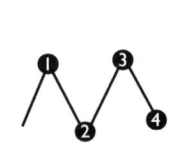

The third is major and happy.

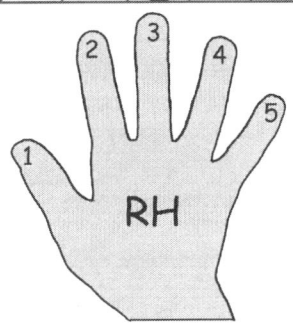

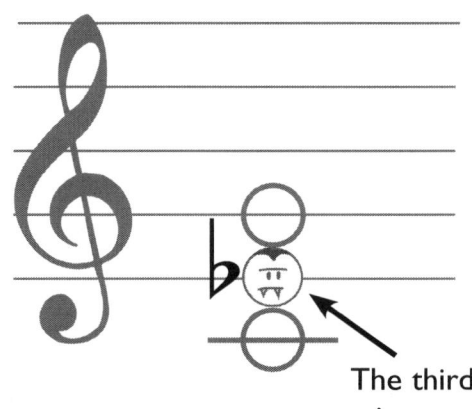

Bring the third (E) down to E♭

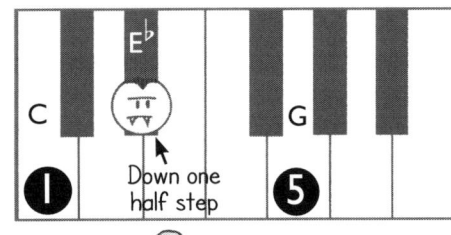
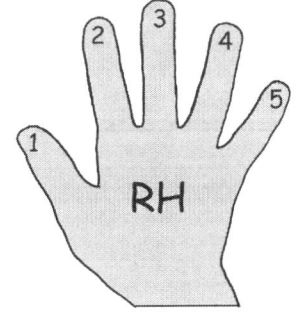

The third is minor or sad and mysterious.

Major and Minor Chords

44 DOWNWARD SHIFT

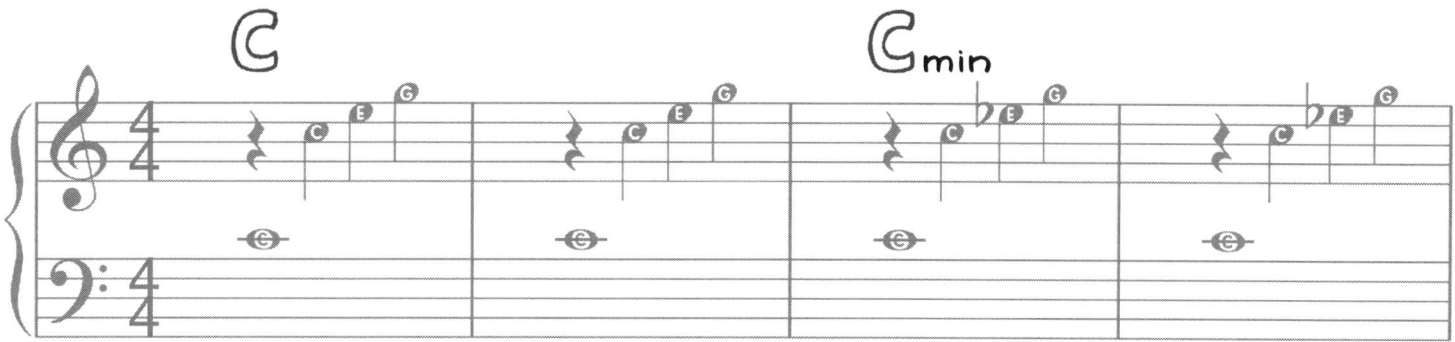
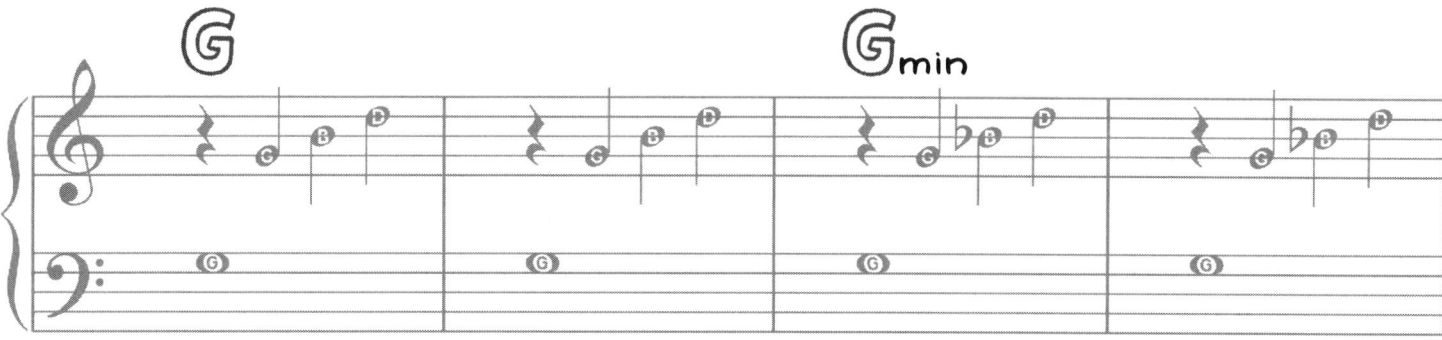

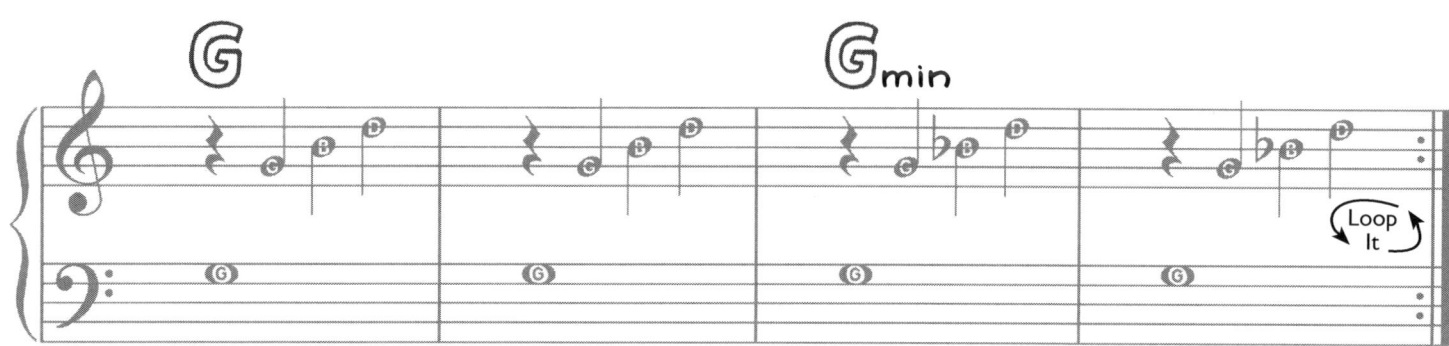

Major and Minor Chords

MINOR TO MAJOR (CHEER IT UP...)

LET'S CHANGE A MINOR INTO A MAJOR...

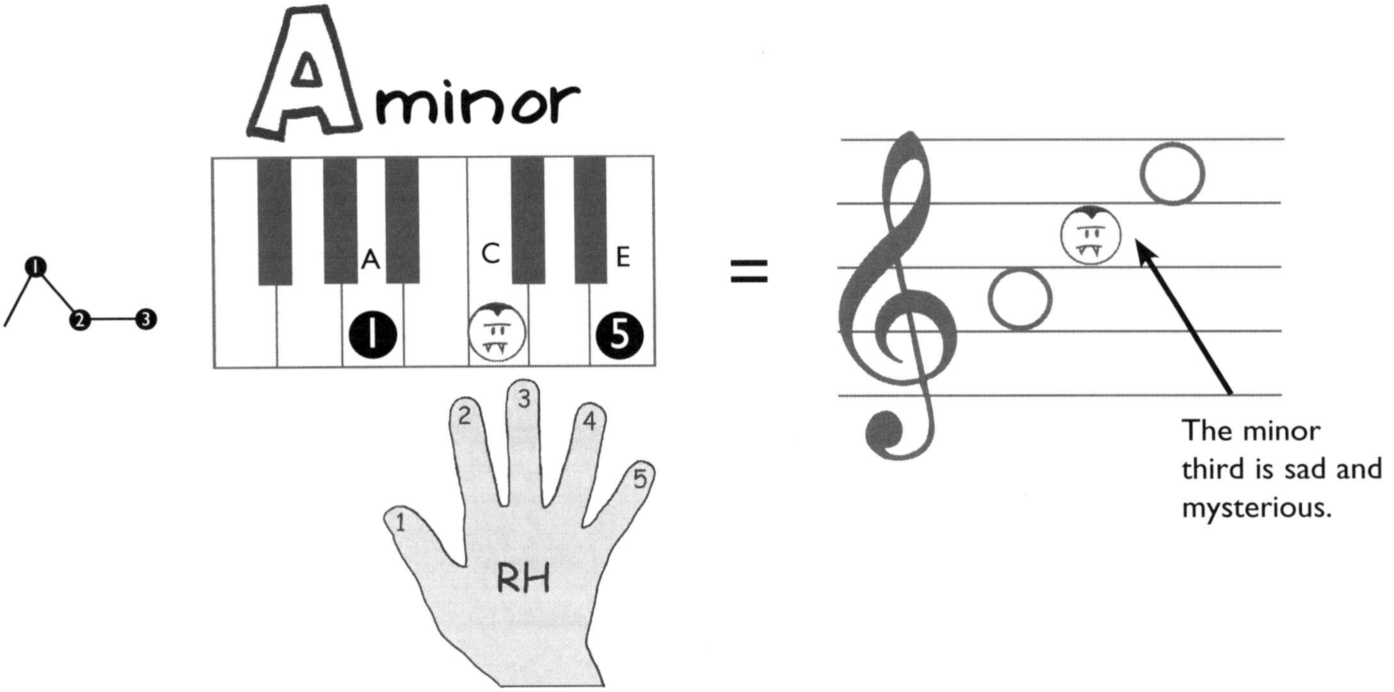

A minor

The minor third is sad and mysterious.

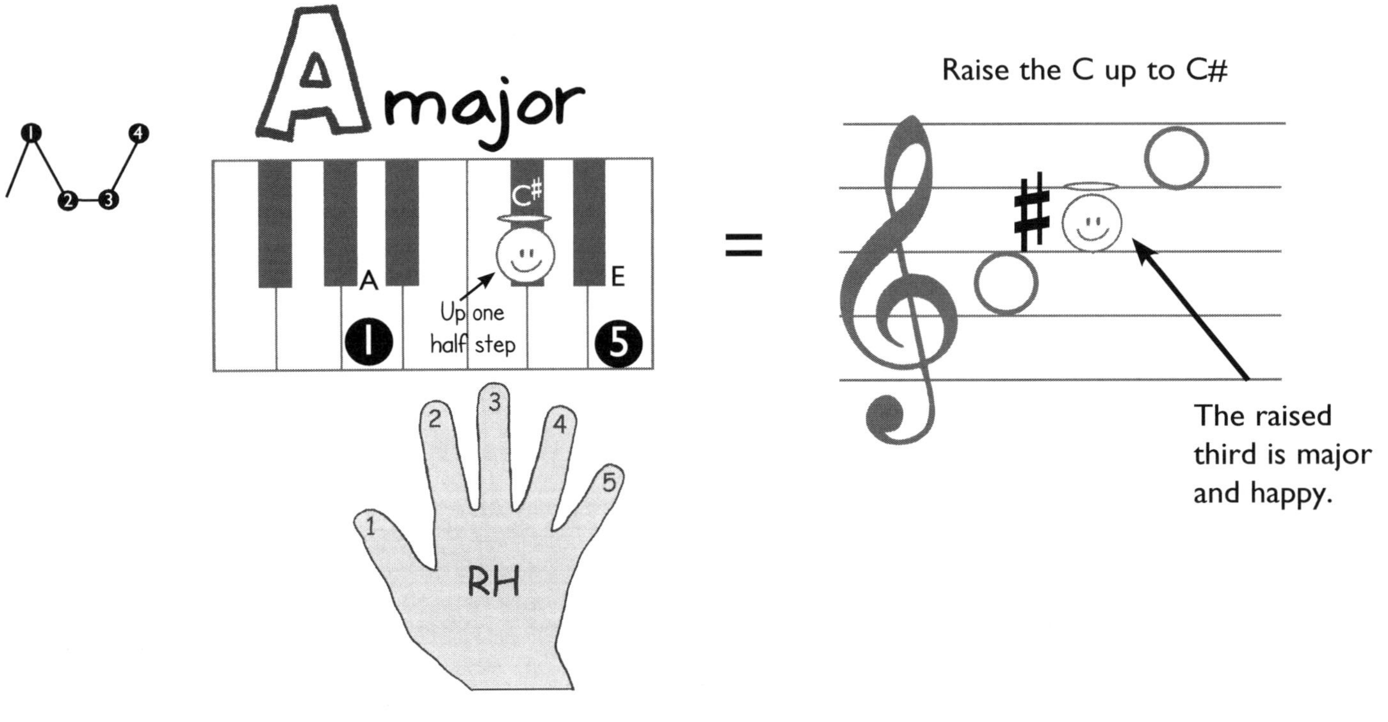

A major

Raise the C up to C#

The raised third is major and happy.

84 — Major and Minor Chords

45 UPWARD BOUND

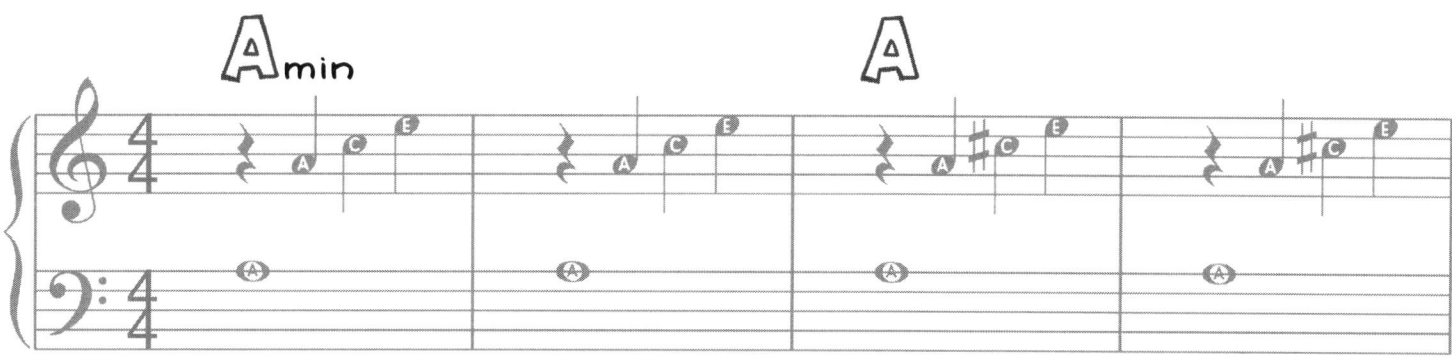
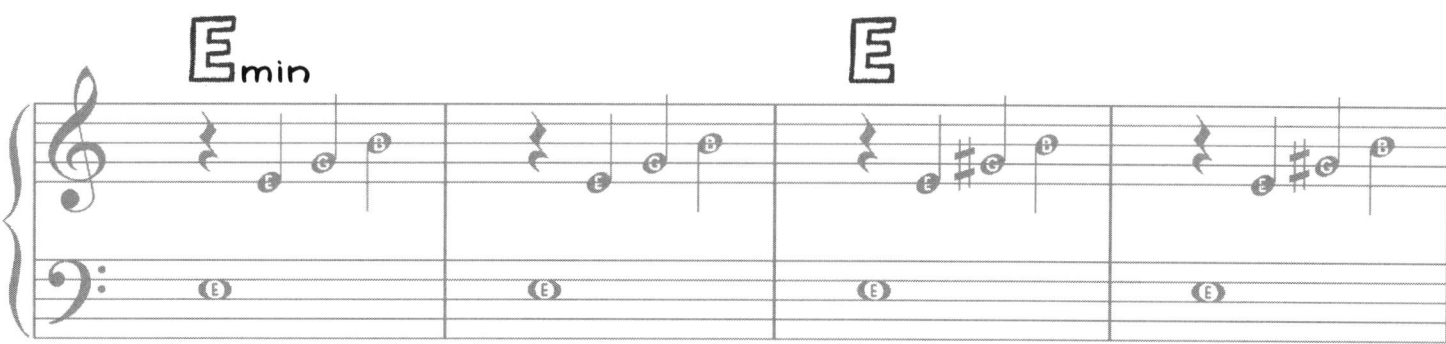
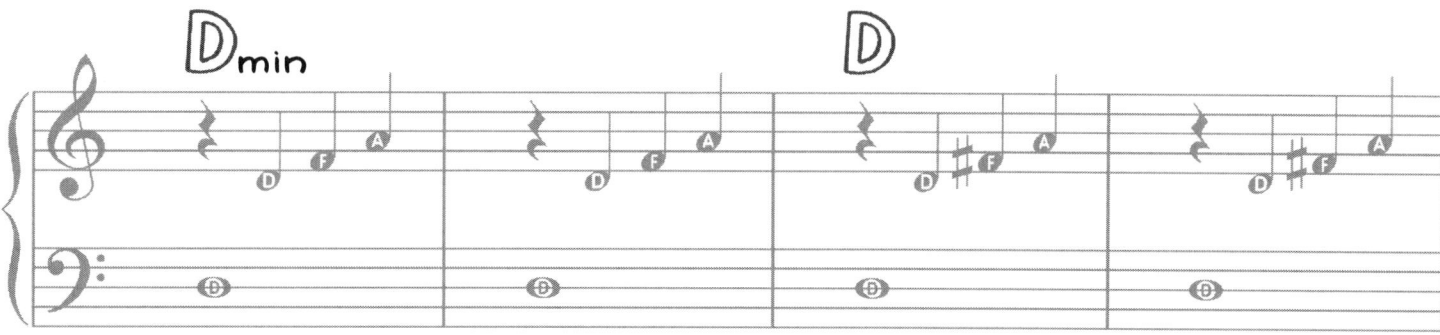
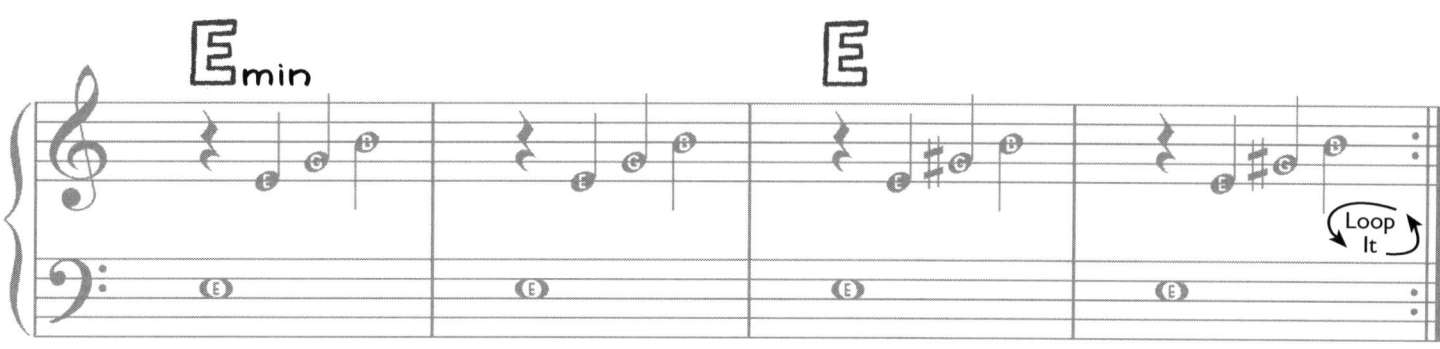

Major and Minor Chords

46 MALAGUENA MASTERPIECE

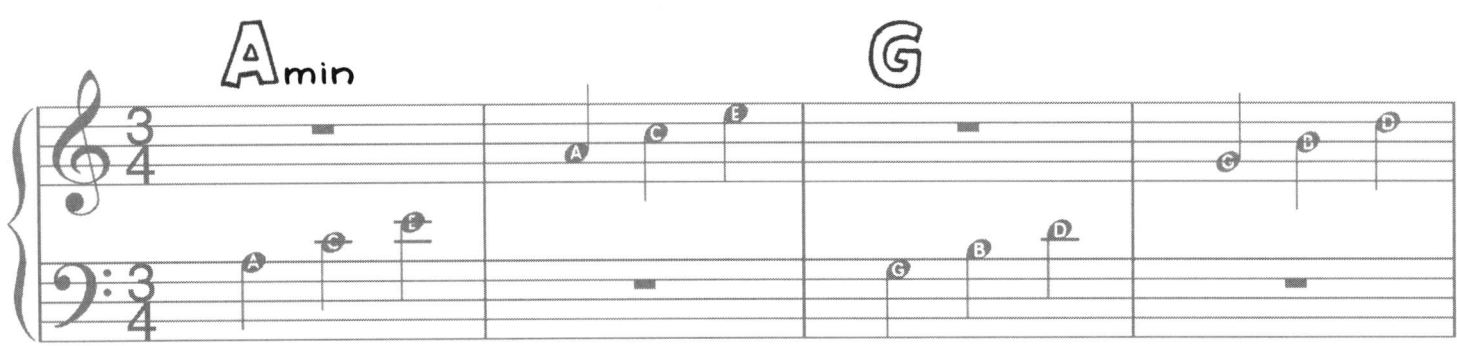

KNOWLEDGE!

You now understand major and minor – a major theory concept.

Review: A major chord has ____ half-steps between the root and the third.

A minor chord has ____ half steps between the root and the third.

KNOWLEDGE

Major and Minor Chords

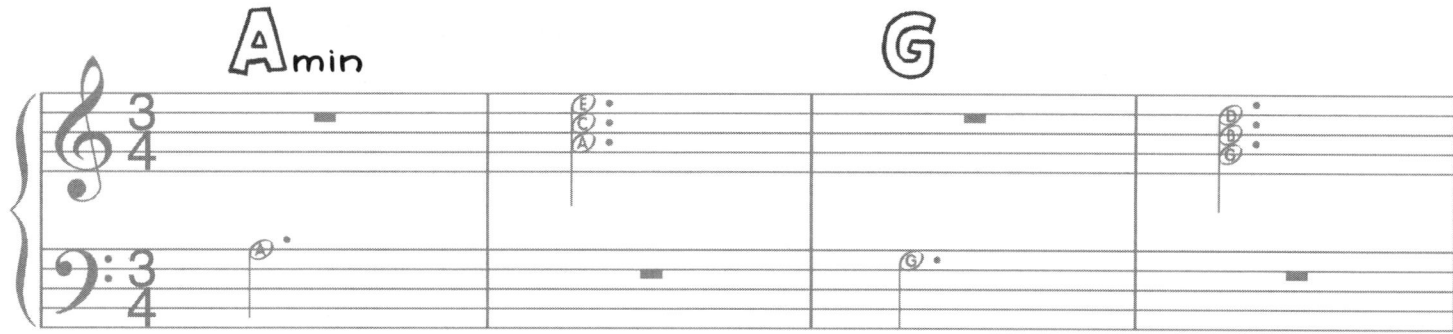

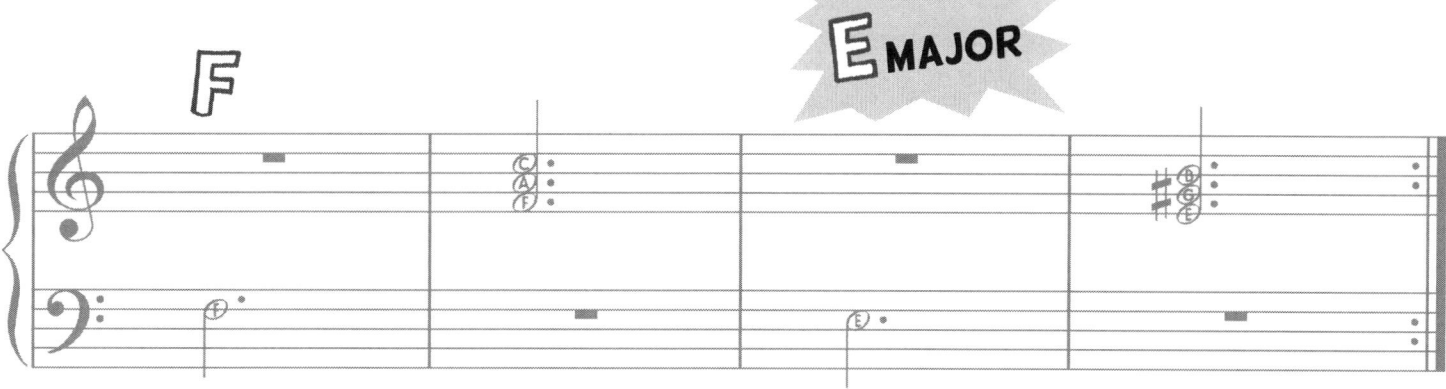

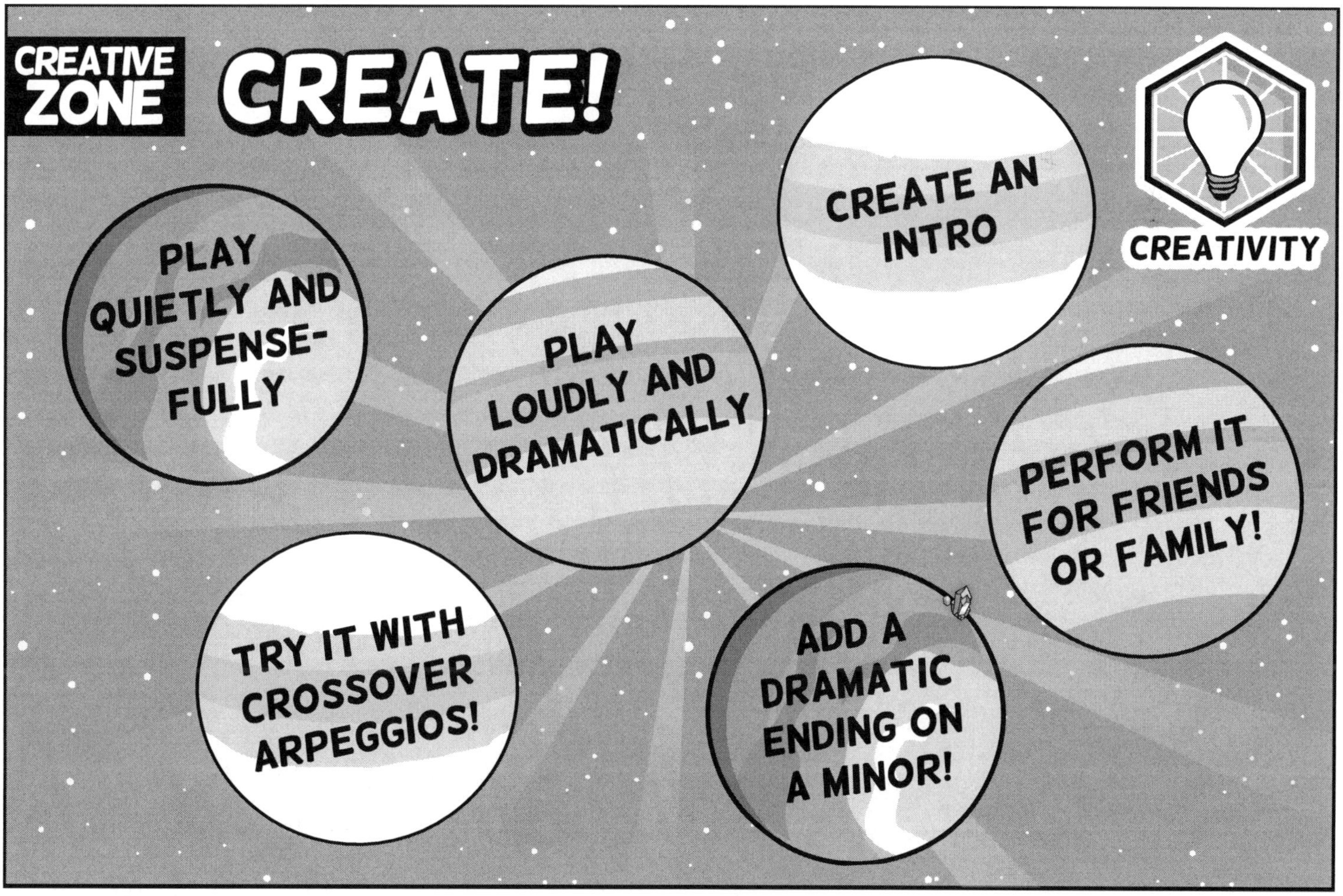

CREATIVE ZONE: CREATE!

- PLAY QUIETLY AND SUSPENSEFULLY
- PLAY LOUDLY AND DRAMATICALLY
- CREATE AN INTRO
- PERFORM IT FOR FRIENDS OR FAMILY!
- TRY IT WITH CROSSOVER ARPEGGIOS!
- ADD A DRAMATIC ENDING ON A MINOR!

CREATIVITY

Major and Minor Chords

QUANTUM QUIZ!

FOR THIS QUIZ, COMPLETE THIS GAME IN ONE (OR ALL!) OF THE WAYS LISTED:

- Build a major and then a minor chord on that root note. Repeat!
- Roll the dice, then build a major and minor chord on that root note.
- Hint: Remember, some minor chords (Am, Em, Dm) use all white keys. Count steps to build your chords — don't rely on the color of the keys!

COMPLETE! ☐

Game board path: A → C → D → E → G → F → C → E → G → A → F → C → CHOOSE A ROOT NOTE!

COMMAND CENTER

Pattern Powers

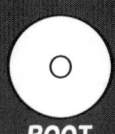 ROOT
 ARPEGGIO
 MALAGUENA POWER PROGRESSION
 CHORDS
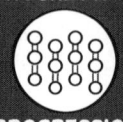 PROGRESSION
 PACHELBEL POWER PROGRESSION
 CROSSOVER ARPEGGIOS
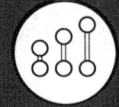 INTERVALS
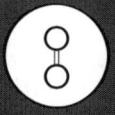 FIFTHS
 MAJOR/MINOR

Creative Powers

 EXPLORE
 CREATIVITY
 LISTENING
 EXPERIMENT
 ARTISTRY
 PERFORMANCE
 IMPROVISE
 RHYTHM
 KNOWLEDGE
 SONGWRITING

"Congratulations! You've earned the powers of Knowledge and Major/Minor."

"Majorly amazing!"

"Let's perform!"

Major and Minor Chords

© 2020 Meridee Winters ® All Rights Reserved.

CHAPTER 9
MAJOR MINOR CONCERTO

Welcome to the concert the whole galaxy has been talking about, starring... you!

At this stop on your Chord Quest, you'll be mustering your courage, applying all you've learned and performing some epic songs! (Psst! The performance practice will come in handy during your final challenge next chapter!)

Let's play!

47 MAJOR MINOR CONCERTO: ARPEGGIOS

Major Minor Concerto

48 MAJOR MINOR CONCERTO: CHORDS

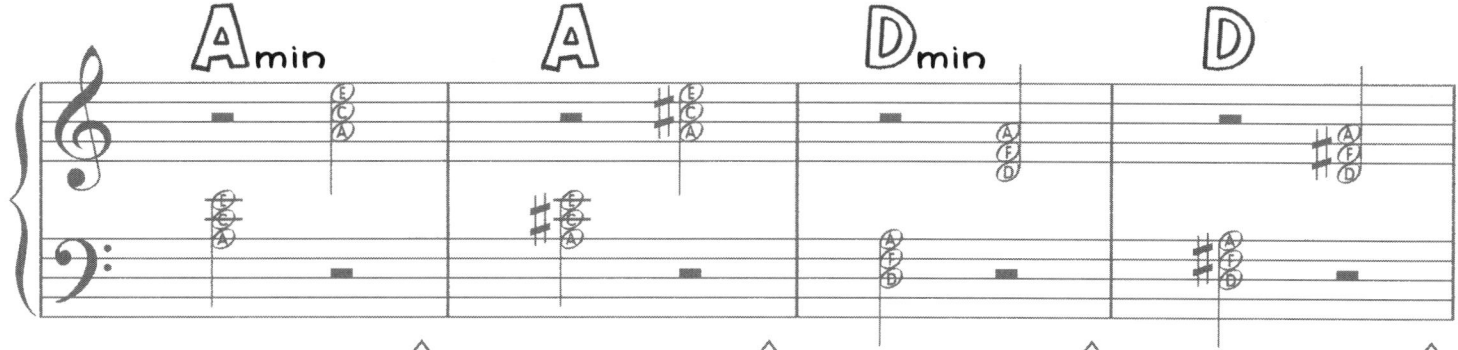

Repeat G Major again

Now go back and play Exercise 46 for a big finish!

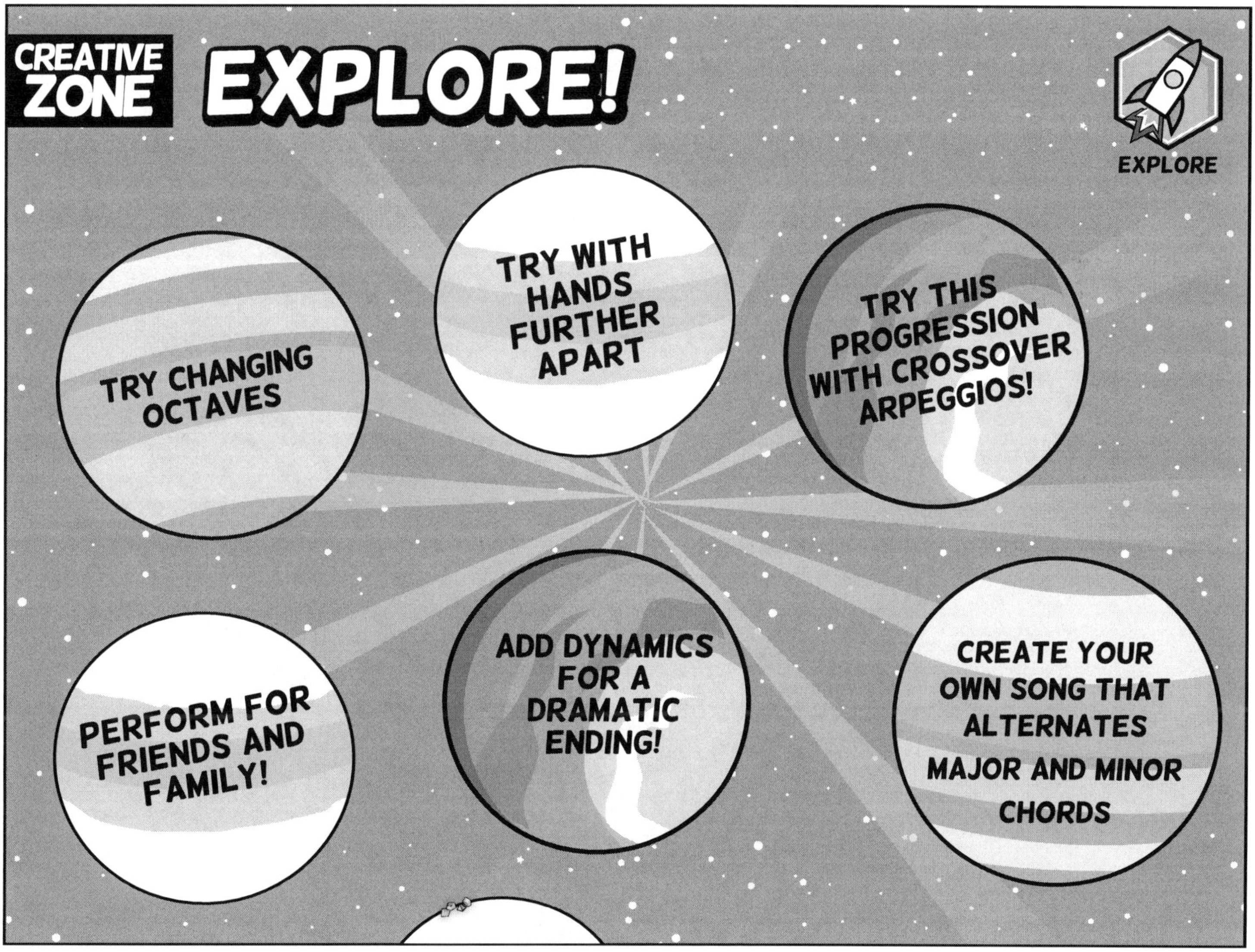

CREATIVE ZONE: EXPLORE!

- TRY CHANGING OCTAVES
- TRY WITH HANDS FURTHER APART
- TRY THIS PROGRESSION WITH CROSSOVER ARPEGGIOS!
- PERFORM FOR FRIENDS AND FAMILY!
- ADD DYNAMICS FOR A DRAMATIC ENDING!
- CREATE YOUR OWN SONG THAT ALTERNATES MAJOR AND MINOR CHORDS

Major Minor Concerto

 # QUANTUM QUIZ!

1. PLAY!
PLAY THE MAJOR MINOR CONCERTO FROM MEMORY. ADD FEELING!

COMPLETE! ☐

2. PREPARE
YOUR CHORD QUEST TEST IS NEXT! ARE YOU READY? LIST ANY AREAS THAT MIGHT NEED REVIEW HERE, AND THEN GO BACK AND REFRESH.

The moment is here! You put on a great concert and are ready for your Chord Quest Test. Then you'll earn your last power.

AND DEFEAT PROFESSOR PERFECTO!

COMMAND CENTER

Pattern Powers

 ROOT    ARPEGGIO

 POWER PROGRESSION    CHORDS

 PROGRESSION    POWER PROGRESSION (PACHELBEL)

 CROSSOVER ARPEGGIOS    INTERVALS

 FIFTHS    MAJOR/MINOR

Creative Powers

 EXPLORE    CREATIVITY

 LISTENING    EXPERIMENT

 ARTISTRY    PERFORMANCE

IMPROVISE   RHYTHM

 KNOWLEDGE   SONGWRITING

Major Minor Concerto

CHAPTER 10
CHORD QUEST TEST

You've done it! You've earned so many powers (just one left!), and officially ready for the Chord Quest Test!

To complete this test, you will need to use all the skills you've learned to create your own song. Then, you'll need to transmit a song into the universe (and also directly to two people you know who could use a musical day-brightener). Once you broadcast your song, hopefully the signal is strong enough to reach Perfecto Piano Music School on Planet Blah. If it is, the students will be able to hear your creativity, pack up their perfectionism and break out of their blah-ness.

Are you ready for your test?

CHORD QUEST TEST

You've completed your training in Meridee Winters Chord Quest Powerful Piano Lessons Level 1, and are now ready for your Chord Quest test. If you can prove your knowledge, earn your Songwriting Power and defeat Professor Perfecto, your quest will be complete. Then you'll portal to Level 2! Are you ready?

1. REFLECT AND PREPARE:

COMPLETE! ☐

1. Reflect on all the skills you've gained along this Chord Quest.
2. Color in the badges on this pages as you think back on the lessons learned.

PATTERN POWERS
- ROOT
- ARPEGGIO
- CHORDS
- PROGRESSION
- INTERVALS
- MALAGUENA POWER PROGRESSION
- FIFTHS
- PACHELBEL POWER PROGRESSION
- MAJOR/MINOR
- CROSSOVER ARPEGGIOS

CREATIVE POWERS
- EXPLORE
- CREATIVITY
- LISTENING
- EXPERIMENT
- ARTISTRY
- PERFORMANCE
- IMPROVISE
- RHYTHM
- KNOWLEDGE
- SONGWRITING

 For the first part of your test, review your powers on the left page and complete the challenges below.

PROVE YOUR:
- KNOWLEDGE
- PERFORMANCE SKILLS
- MEMORY

AND THEN...

YOU'LL HEAD TO THE SONGWRITING LAB!

2. PROVE YOUR KNOWLEDGE
BY ANSWERING THESE QUESTIONS...

What is a chord progression?
_____

COMPLETE! ☐

Prove your interval knowledge: play a 2nd, 3rd, 4th and 5th

COMPLETE! ☐

Prove your major and minor chord knowledge: play a major chord, and then a minor one.

COMPLETE! ☐

3. PERFORM YOUR FAVORITE PIECE FROM THIS BOOK WITH ARTISTRY AND DYNAMICS

Title:
_____

Comments/Notes:
_____
_____
_____

COMPLETE! ☐

4. PLAY FROM MEMORY

Perform the progression from Pachelbel's Canon with at least three different pattern combinations. It must be smooth and have style.

COMPLETE! ☐

WELCOME TO THE SONGWRITING LAB!

You've earned so many pattern powers...

And creative powers!

Pick a progression!

- C G F G
- C A_m F G
- C G A_m F
- A_m F C G
- C E_m F G
- F G E_m F
- A_m G F E_m

PICK A PATTERN

- Root, Arpeggio
- Arpeggio, Arpeggio
- Chord, Chord
- Root, Root, Chord, Chord
- Melodic Fifths

Chord Quest Test

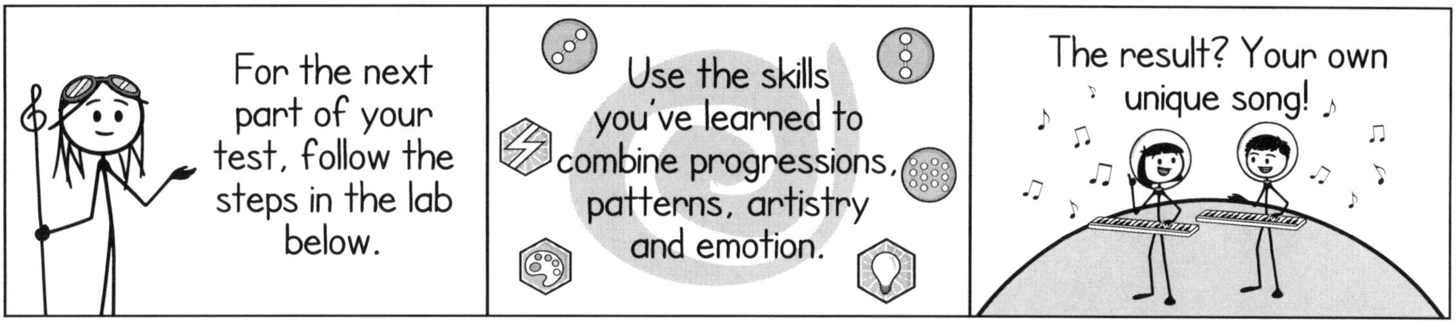

 For the next part of your test, follow the steps in the lab below.

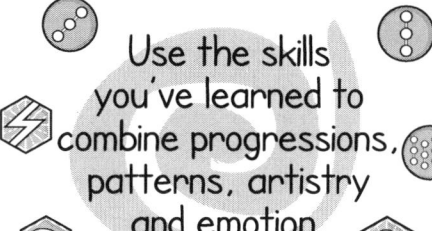 Use the skills you've learned to combine progressions, patterns, artistry and emotion.

 The result? Your own unique song!

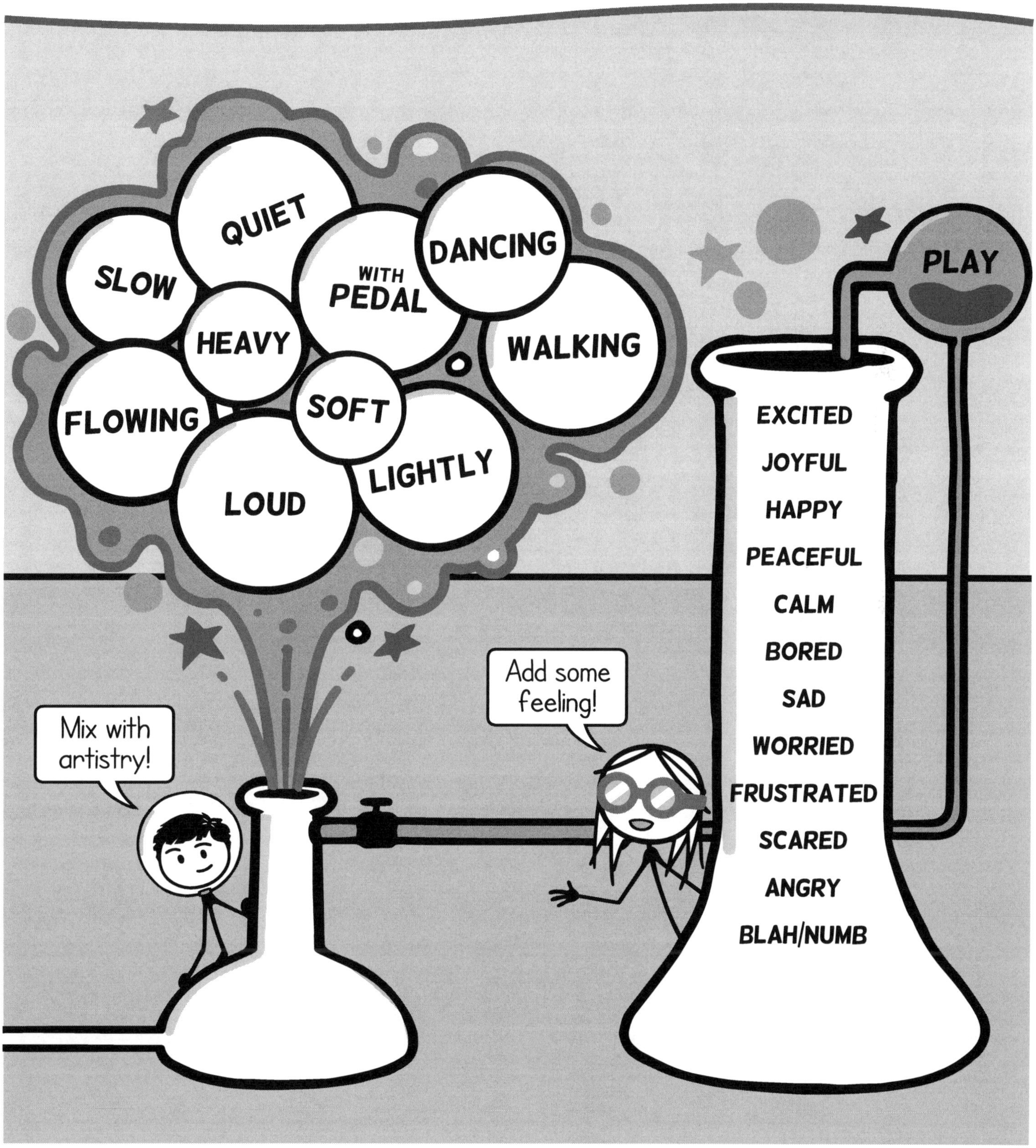

Chord Quest Test

WRITE DOWN YOUR CREATIONS

Write down the creations and songs your created in the composer's lab here. You can include progressions, patterns, lyrics and more. Come back to the Songwriting Lab again and again to create more music!

You've earned the last power - the SONGWRITING POWER!

Chord Quest Test

SNEAK PEEK

CHAPTER 4: OOM PAH

DO YOU KNOW HOW MANY TYPES OF MUSIC USE OOM-PAH PATTERNS?

"Ragtime, European Waltzes..."

"And circus music!"

AND COMPOSERS LIKE

"Chopin"

"Strauss"

"Willy Wonka!"

Many of us think of Oom-pah music and respond with a smile — imagining polka bands, circus music or, of course, the Oompa Loompas from Willy Wonka's Chocolate Factory.

But the Oom-pah pattern is full of even more surprises. It is a true power pattern used in a wide variety of styles and has a rich history. Eastern European classical composers like Strauss, Brahms and Chopin all used Oom-pah patterns in their waltzes. A popular style of Klezmer music (a traditional Jewish style) came out of this same part of the world, and also shows an Oom-pah influence.

The Oom-pah list goes on and on. Ragtime players used it. Even famous composer Danny Elfman (who has written the soundtracks for TONS of movies... including the Simpsons' theme song!) uses Oom-pah... and so can you!

EARN POWERS to DEFEAT the Baron von Boring and the forces of BLAH!

Now that you've completed Chord Quest Level One, let's take a look at what you'll learn next! Chord Quest Powerful Piano Lessons Level Two teaches many more great skills, such as:

- Two-Handed Patterns
- Rockin' Rhythms
- Lead Sheet Reading
- Transposition
- Classical Patterns
- And Much More!

Book Two also gets whimsical and teaches Oom-Pah music. Let's take a sneak peak at an Oom-pah pattern, done in the Klezmer style - a famous style of music that's centuries old!

Sneak Peek

KLEZMERIZED

LEFT HAND

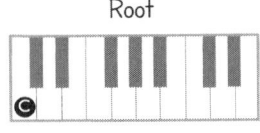

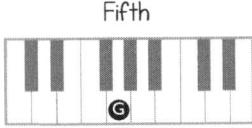

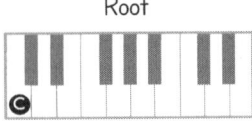

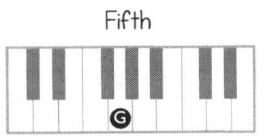

RIGHT HAND

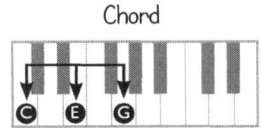

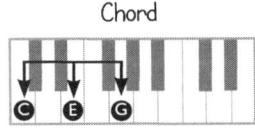

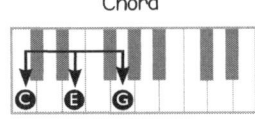

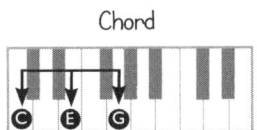

- On beat one, the left hand plays the root note.
- On beat two, the right hand plays the chord.
- On beat three, the left hand plays the <u>fifth</u>.
- On beat four, the right hand plays the chord again.
- Repeat the pattern.

PRACTICE IN C POSITION UNTIL SMOOTH

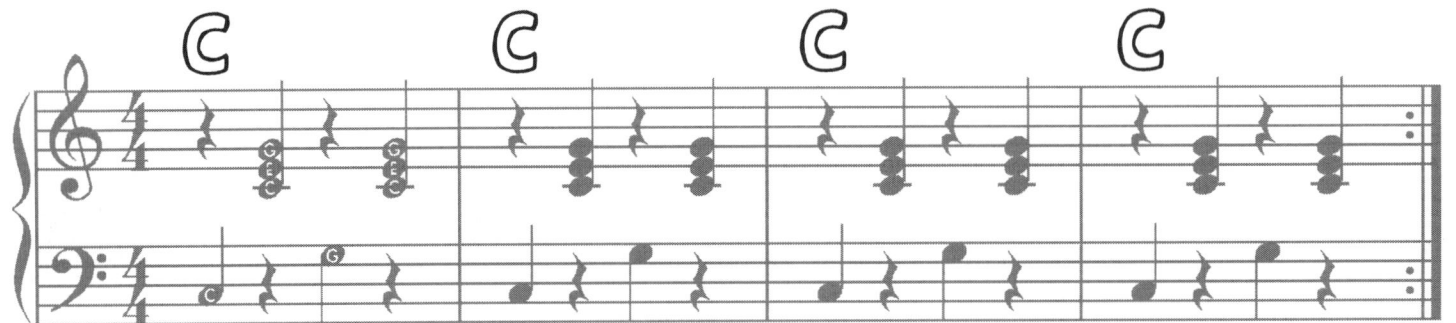

Sneak Peek

30. KLEZMERIZED

Play the E major chord instead of E minor. Just play a G# instead of G every time. It's been Klezmerized!

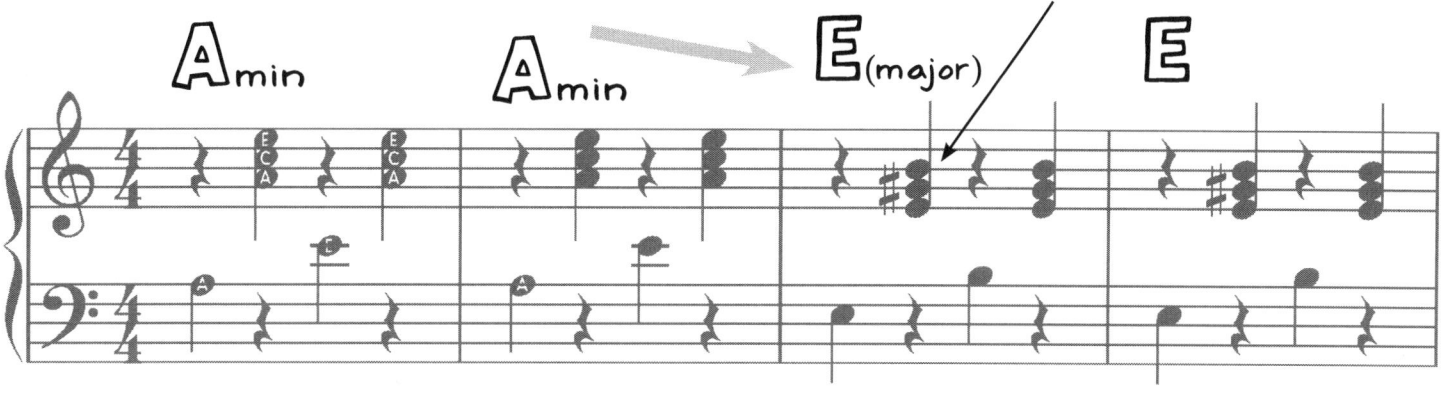
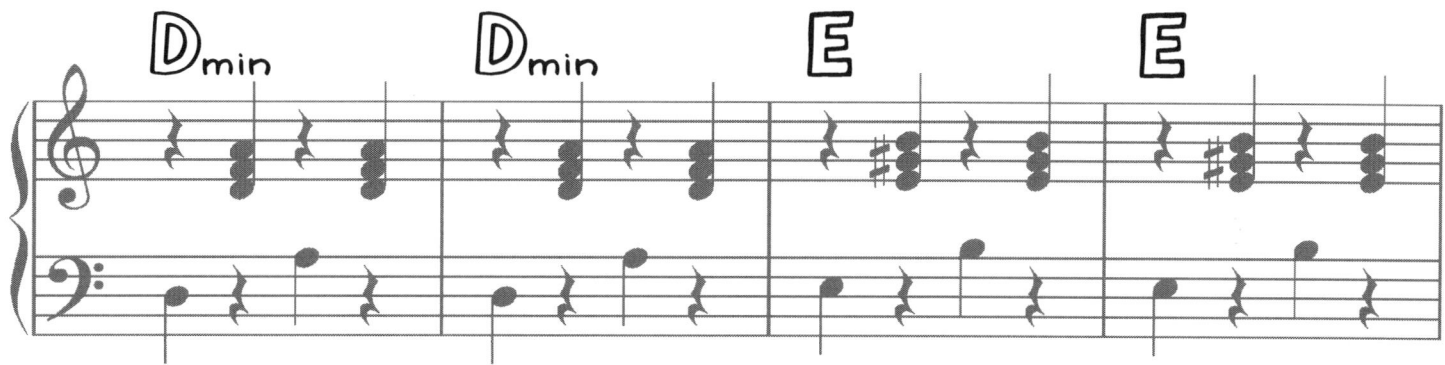
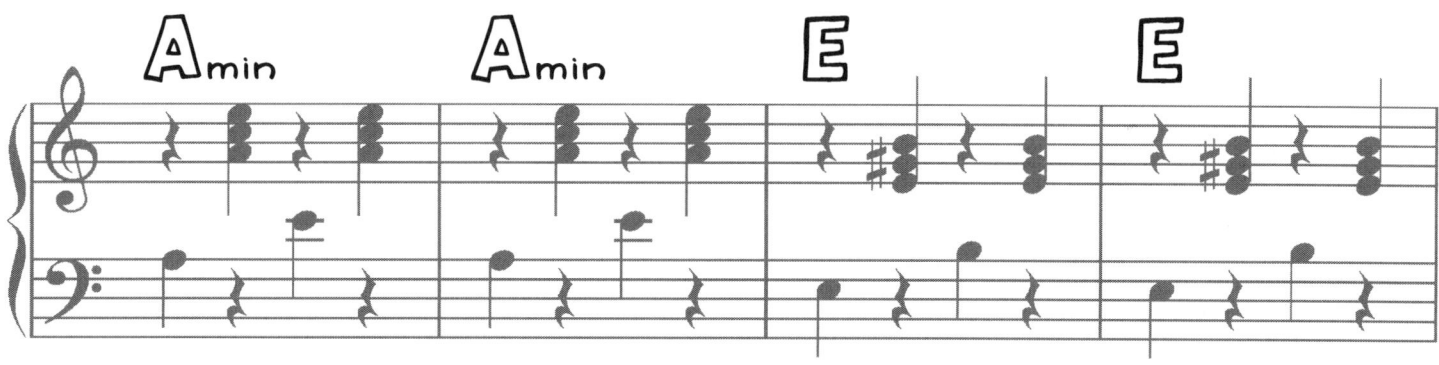
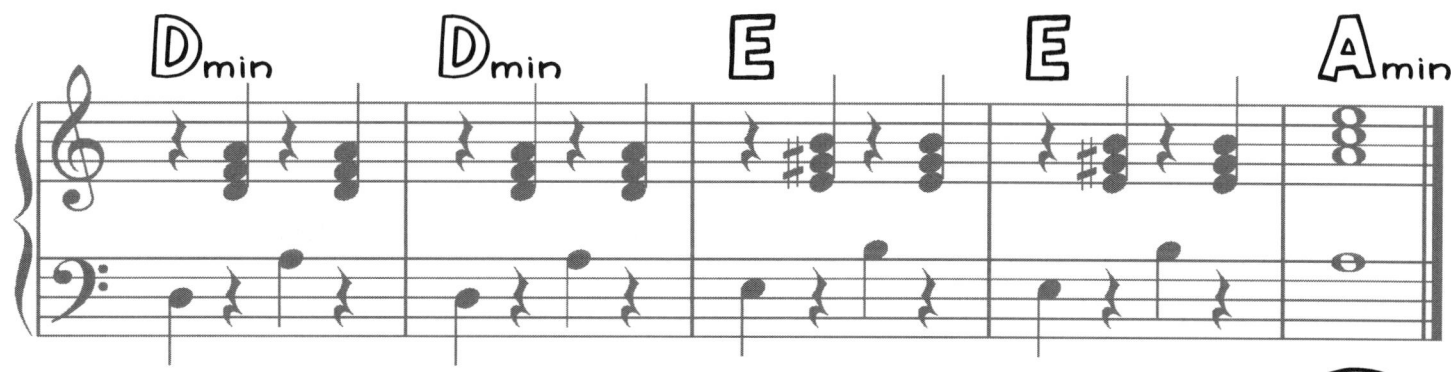

Look at and listen to Klezmer music online.

Sneak Peek

THE MERIDEE WINTERS MUSIC METHOD
Sparking brilliance with patterns, chords and games

Want to supercharge your progress with your instrument or find a tool to help you create music?
Find Meridee's globally-popular, trailblazing instructional books, innovative music games, online lesson info and more at merideewintersmusicmethod.com – or find us on Amazon.com!

CHORD QUEST SERIES

Our brains are wired to excel at patterns. Finally, a kid's music book that teaches that way. (And sure has fun doing it.)

What do you get when you take the great content and innovative teaching style from *Chord Crash Course*, but design and pace it for school aged kids? The *Chord Quest Powerful Piano Lessons* Series! Like its older counterpart, *Chord Quest* uses the power of patterns and shapes to have students playing great-sounding music from the very first lesson — without reading music. **Each book is its own quest where students learn universal patterns, earn powers and defeat villains like the Baron von Boring!**

SUPER START! MY FIRST PIANO PATTERNS

Early childhood is a "magic window" for learning language – and young kids shouldn't wait to learn the language of music. "Super Start! My First Piano Patterns" teaches young beginners in the way their brains learn best – through patterns and play.

Super Start! My First Piano Patterns contains 36 piano pattern songs, games and activities- that will guarantee a fun and successful start to piano lessons. As students work their way across Planet Plunk they learn, play, improvise, explore and even encounter a few "Plunkadillos." By using patterns, simple diagrams and playful characters, students sound great from day one – without needing to read music. Songs gradually increase in skill throughout the book, culminating in a final chapter of youngster-friendly waltzes and classically-inspired pattern songs. **Sound great! Play by shape!**

Meridee Winters Music Method ★ merideewintersmusicmethod.com

Made in the USA
Middletown, DE
30 August 2021